the literary terms handbook

An Easy-to-Use Source of Definitions, Examples, and Exercises for Students and Teachers

Sunflower
education
Exceptional Books for Teachers and Parents™

A Great Way to Teach Literature!

Literary terms are the building blocks of literature. Give students a firm grasp of them with this well thought out handbook that features an in-depth look at 29 literary terms. Each lesson follows an easy-to-use format: a definition of the term is followed by a discussion using two excellent examples in prose or poetry. Questions promote and ensure understanding. A writing exercise for each term provides an opportunity for application. Gives students the knowledge and experience to interpret literature with confidence!

Grades 9-12. Meets National Council of Teachers of English/International Reading Association Standards for the English Language Arts.

58 Pages of Activity Sheets • Complete Answer Key

Please feel free to photocopy the activity sheets in this book within reason. Sunflower Education grants teachers permission to photocopy the activity sheets from this book for educational use. This permission is granted to individual teachers and not entire schools or school systems. Please send any permissions questions to permissions@SunflowerEducation.net.

Visit **SunflowerEducation.Net** for more great books!

Editorial   Sunflower Education, Mirielle Clifford

Design   Blue Agave Studio

ISBN-13: 978-1-937166-11-3
ISBN-10: 1-937166-11-2

CONTENTS

To The Teacher

Welcome to *The Literary Terms Handbook: An Easy-to-Use Source of Definitions, Examples, and Exercises for Students and Teachers.* This book was written with the belief that literature is fun, and it is designed to inspire and maintain a love of literature in your students.

Literary Terms: The Key to Literature

Literary terms are also known as literary elements because they are the building blocks of literature. They apply to all kinds of literary works. A firm grasp of these elements will help students analyze the works they read and improve the works they write. Terms in this book range from the technical, such as meter, to the more conceptual, like symbolism. All are essential keys for unlocking an author's intent in any story or poem.

The Literary Terms Handbook: A Teacher and Student-Friendly Tool

This book is designed to strengthen your students' grasp of literary elements. *The Literary Terms Handbook* offers an in-depth look at 29 different elements in a way that lets students focus on each one individually.

How This Book Is Organized Each lesson follows an easy-to-use format featuring a definition of the term and two examples of that term from outstanding pieces of prose or poetry. Each lesson also includes four questions and a writing exercise to ensure students' understanding. Answers to these questions can be found in the Answer Key. Terms in boldface have their own lessons.

How to Use This Book *The Literary Terms Handbook* will easily fit into any classroom or homeschooling routine. You may wish to use this book to accompany a particular text your students are reading or with a particular writing unit they are working on. You may also wish to use this book on its own. Here is a suggested lesson cycle to follow for each term:

- **Introduce:** Read each definition aloud. Invite students to identify examples of the term in use. Ask: what is the value of this concept in creating and understanding literature?

- **Discuss:** Discuss the examples in the introductory essay. Encourage students to ask questions. Ensure that they understand the examples themselves, as well as understand how they relate to the literary element they illustrate.

- **Explore:** Ask your students why they think that literary element is important. Find examples of it in other texts, or have students come up with their own versions of the element.

- **Evaluate:** Have students answer the questions at the end of each section, either on their own or with a group.

Why Study Literary Terms? Invariably, high school students ask, "when will I use this?" They wonder how the work they do in school will help them in the real world.

The Literary Terms Handbook is meant to be useful for students as they continue in their studies and work. Studying literary terms will improve their critical thinking skills. When students can analyze a poem, it ceases to be a blur of words, and students are able to ask questions that are to-the-point and effective. Their communication skills are enhanced as they learn how to decipher others' meaning.

The Literary Terms Handbook addresses the National Council of Teachers of English/International Reading Association Standards for the English Language Arts. These standards equip students with real-life communication skills, helping them to become independent, critical thinkers.

Now that you know a little bit about *The Literary Terms Handbook*, you're ready to begin! We wish you luck as you share the wonders of literature with your students.

"The answers you get from literature depend on the questions you pose."

—Margaret Atwood

National Council of Teachers of English / International Reading Association Standards for the English Language Arts

1. Students read a wide range of print and non-print texts to build an understanding of texts, of themselves, and of the cultures of the United States and the world; to acquire new information; to respond to the needs and demands of society and the workplace; and for personal fulfillment. Among these texts are fiction and nonfiction, classic and contemporary works.
2. Students read a wide range of literature from many periods in many genres to build an understanding of the many dimensions (e.g., philosophical, ethical, aesthetic) of human experience.
3. Students apply a wide range of strategies to comprehend, interpret, evaluate, and appreciate texts. They draw on their prior experience, their interactions with other readers and writers, their knowledge of word meaning and of other texts, their word identification strategies, and their understanding of textual features (e.g., sound-letter correspondence, sentence structure, context, graphics).
4. Students adjust their use of spoken, written, and visual language (e.g., conventions, style, vocabulary) to communicate effectively with a variety of audiences and for different purposes.
5. Students employ a wide range of strategies as they write and use different writing process elements appropriately to communicate with different audiences for a variety of purposes.
6. Students apply knowledge of language structure, language conventions (e.g., spelling and punctuation), media techniques, figurative language, and genre to create, critique, and discuss print and non-print texts.
7. Students conduct research on issues and interests by generating ideas and questions, and by posing problems. They gather, evaluate, and synthesize data from a variety of sources (e.g., print and non-print texts, artifacts, people) to communicate their discoveries in ways that suit their purpose and audience.
8. Students use a variety of technological and information resources (e.g., libraries, databases, computer networks, video) to gather and synthesize information and to create and communicate knowledge.
9. Students develop an understanding of and respect for diversity in language use, patterns, and dialects across cultures, ethnic groups, geographic regions, and social roles.
10. Students whose first language is not English make use of their first language to develop competency in the English language arts and to develop understanding of content across the curriculum.
11. Students participate as knowledgeable, reflective, creative, and critical members of a variety of literacy communities.
12. Students use spoken, written, and visual language to accomplish their own purposes (e.g., for learning, enjoyment, persuasion, and the exchange of information).

Literary Element Lesson		NCTE/IRA Standards Addressed
1	Allegory	1-6, 11, 12
2	Alliteration	1-8, 11, 12
3	Allusion	1-8, 11, 12
4	Analogy	1-6, 11, 12
5	Assonance	1-6, 11, 12
6	Atmosphere	1-6, 11, 12
7	Ballad	1-6, 11
8	Characterization	1-6, 12
9	Couplet	1-6, 11, 12
10	Figurative Language	1-6, 11, 12
11	Foreshadowing	1-6, 11, 12
12	Imagery	1-6, 11
13	Inversion	1-6, 11, 12
14	Irony	1-6, 11, 12
15	Metaphor	1-6, 11, 12
16	Meter	1-6, 11, 12
17	Onomatopoeia	1-6, 11, 12
18	Personification	1-6, 11,
19	Plot	1-6, 11, 12
20	Point of View	1-6, 11, 12
21	Refrain	1-6, 11, 12
22	Rhyme	1-6, 11, 12
23	Rhythm	1-6, 11, 12
24	Simile	1-6, 11, 12
25	Sonnet	1-6, 11, 12
26	Style	1-6, 11
27	Symbolism	1-6, 11, 12
28	Theme	1-6, 11, 12
29	Tone	1-6, 11, 12

Answer Key

1. Allegory

1. *Answers will vary.* <u>**Possible answer:**</u> The dark forest represents the path away from God, and toward sin.
2. *Answers will vary.* <u>**Possible answer:**</u> When Dante "abandoned the true way," he was not paying attention to his actions, as if he were asleep.
3. *Answers will vary.* <u>**Possible answer:**</u> The tornado represents a tour-de-force that robs people of everything they have. This catastrophe could be natural or man-made.
4. *Answers will vary.* <u>**Possible answer:**</u> It's a fitting symbol. At first, it's surprising that Guthrie would liken the actions of that "somebody else," a person, to a natural phenomenon. Maybe he does this on purpose, though, because a person who could take someone's life away would have to be unfeeling.
5. *Answers will vary.* <u>**Possible answer:**</u> Allegories are more accessible and personal than moral treatises are. People can relate to them, and they might learn more from a story about people than from a commandment or a philosophical discourse. It is almost a way to "sneak" a lesson into a piece of writing.

2. Alliteration

1. *Answers will vary.* <u>**Possible answer:**</u> Before Newton, it was difficult to "see," or understand, the laws of nature, so they might as well have been in the dark. Newton's discoveries about light were spectacular.
2. *Answers will vary.* <u>**Possible answer:**</u> Yes, because the alliteration is a sound-based technique.
3. *Answers will vary.*
4. Students, through memorizing this speech, should hear how Shakespeare uses alliteration.
5. *Answers will vary.* Students should use alliteration at least three times.

3. Allusion

1. *Answers will vary.* <u>**Possible answer:**</u> Maeterlinck is saying that even though we change as time progresses we're always essentially the same person. Your past actions will always be there even if you try to walk away from them.
2. *Answers will vary.* Students' answers should mention Daedalus's status as a master craftsman and inventor. Answers might also refer to Daedalus's role in creating a labyrinth to contain a Minotaur. <u>**Possible answer:**</u> Perhaps Stephen, like Daedalus, is an inventor and is creative. If Stephen is a poet, then he must be inventive with words. Also, maybe Stephen ends up confusing himself with his words and literary creations, as if he were in a labyrinth.
3. *Answers will vary.* <u>**Possible answer:**</u> According to the poem, the "houses" of moral people are ugly and boring in comparison to the "shining palace" built on an unstable foundation.
4. *Answers will vary.* Students should use examples from "The Second Fig" and the Ulysses excerpt. <u>**Possible answer:**</u> Direct and indirect allusions could affect readers differently, depending on how familiar they are with the source of the allusion. If someone read "Second Fig," and didn't know that it directly alluded to the Bible, they would correctly think that rash, exciting people build their houses on sand, while cautious, boring people build on the rock. But they wouldn't know this poem is commenting on issues of morality and religion. So, yes, the indirect allusion in "Second Fig" has a different effect than the one in Ulysses in that respect.
5. *Answers will vary.* Students should use at least three allusions (at least one direct and one indirect).

4. Analogy

1. *Answers will vary.* Students should show they have reflected on what it would be like to have never seen a car before. Students should also demonstrate that they understand analogies well enough to create a few of their own.
2. *Answers will vary.* <u>**Possible answer:**</u> The Martian is awed by how far one can travel with cars, which allows one to see places which would have been too far away before. The Martian is also awed by how quickly cars move.
3. *Answers will vary.* Reward genuine effort. <u>**Possible answer:**</u> These analogies seem appropriate. Perhaps when Williams equates "staying alive" to possessing "a great hall inside of a cell," he is referring to how complex our bodies are. Each one of our cells contains all of our genetic information. When Williams says, "What is it to know? The same root/ underneath the branches" he means we should think critically, or make connections between the things we learn about.
4. *Answers will vary.* <u>**Possible answer:**</u> The analogy in Craig Raine's poem and the analogy about "staying alive" in Williams' poem describe the feeling of being impressed with normal, everyday things. The narrator of Raine's poem is more in awe of technology, and the narrator of Williams' poem is impressed with the human body.
5. *Answers will vary.* Reward genuine effort. Students should use three analogies.

5. Assonance

1. *Answers will vary.* **Possible answer:** The excerpt has a very pleasant sound.
2. *Answers will vary.* **Possible answer:** The repeated vowel sounds capture the feeling of an enchantingly beautiful woman walking, with a light step.
3. Students, through memorizing this verse, should hear how Tennyson uses assonance.
4. *Answers will vary.* **Possible answer:** The effect of the alliteration here is more immediate—it hits you as soon as you read the words. The assonance in "falls" and "walls" has a more delayed, drawling sound.
5. *Answers will vary.* Students should use assonance at least three times.

6. Atmosphere

1. *Answers will vary.* **Possible answer:** The atmosphere of the poem seems hopeful, but not overconfident. All of the characters are beginning something, and they don't know what's going to happen next. There is a sense of anticipation.
2. *Answers will vary.* Students should discuss at least 2 images from the poem. **Possible answer:** The image of the students taking out their pencils has a feeling of nervous but hopeful seriousness. The image of people walking "into that which we cannot yet see" is very intriguing. The reader can visualize people walking forward firmly, progressing, even though they can't see what's in front of them.
3. *Answers will vary.* **Possible answers:** the warm spring, air; the feeling of dawn being near and the war "far away;" the description of the sound of the siren; the dreams of the people still sleeping
4. *Answers will vary.* Students should defend their answers. **Possible answer:** The atmosphere seems appropriate. Nemirovsky does a good job of weaving in the details of an ordinary night with the beginning of an invasion. She's writing about normal people, who are not yet aware of the enormity of what's about to happen.
5. *Answers will vary.* Students should choose an example, describe its atmosphere, say why it had an effect on them, and what that effect was.

7. Ballad

1. *Answers will vary.* **Possible answer:** The repetition of "did fall" makes the ballad sound more songlike.
2. *Answers will vary.* **Possible answer:** Yes, it could be sung easily because it rhymes and alternates between lines that are eight syllables long and those that are six syllables.
3. *Answers will vary.* **Possible answer:** Whereas the atmosphere of "The Bitter Withy" is playful and laid-back, the atmosphere of "The Rime of the Ancient Mariner" is dramatic and captures a stranded sailor's sense of desperation.
4. *Answers will vary.* **Possible answer:** The rhyme in this short poem makes it feel very songlike, like a ballad. It also does tell a story, even though it's not a very plot-driven one. "The Bitter Withy" is not literal, in that Jesus Christ and Mary are normal characters. "An Eastern Ballad," like "The Bitter Withy," is a non-literal, imaginative tale.
5. *Answers will vary.* **Possible answer:** Some poets probably romanticize simpler and more rustic times, when people shared stories with each other despite a lack of traditional education. Art ballads try to capture the atmosphere of those times.

8. Characterization

1. Meets IRA/NCTE Standards 1-3, 6,11. O'Connor tells us what the grandmother looks like when she tells us what she wears. She also describes how the grandmother thinks when the grandmother thinks to herself that "anyone seeing her dead on the highway would know at once that she was a lady.
2. *Answers will vary.* **Possible answer:** O'Connor's tone seems sarcastic, like she's making fun of the grandmother. The old lady acts primly but carries a ridiculous bag that looks like the "head of a hippopotamus." Also, the old lady's thoughts about looking like a lady while being dead on the side of the road are supposed to sound melodramatic.
3. Meets IRA/NCTE Standards 3,4,11. *Answers will vary.* Students should defend their answers. **Possible answer:** It would be surprising if the grandmother changed, but it doesn't seem impossible. I would guess that something dramatic happens to make her change. She appears too settled in her ways to change because of a small incident.
4. *Answers will vary.* **Possible answer:** The end of the passage did surprise me at first, but it makes sense, too. Tolstoy is trying to remind us that even people who seem really important and awe-inspiring are just people. Bolkonsky has small hands and a small stature, so in some ways he isn't too intimidating.
5. *Answers will vary.* Reward genuine effort.

9. Couplet

1. *Answers will vary.* **Possible answer:** We can observe the way the river acts and try to emulate it. We could learn to be strong and calm.
2. *Answers will vary.* **Possible answer:** That person would have depth of thought without unnecessarily confusing, or clouding, him or herself.
3. *Answers will vary.* **Possible answer:** A sun dial is a mathematical creation. The mathematical element in this poem also serves as a contrast to the emotional side of the poem, i.e. the personification and the constancy at night.
4. *Answers will vary.* **Possible answer:** J.V. Cunningham imagines that a sun dial has feelings and a sense of identity. During the day, its shadows are dependent on the sunlight, but at night it's constant. Maybe this constancy at night is peaceful for the sun dial.
5. *Answers will vary.* Reward genuine effort.

10. Figurative Language

1. *Answers will vary.* Students should show an understanding of the simile as a tool for comparing and relating seemingly dissimilar things. **Possible answer:** Porter wants to show that the sun is just waking up and slowly starting to move. This simile is also in keeping with the poem's effort to capture the feeling of the sun being near the earth. If it's resting like a boulder, it's even more solidly on the earth.
2. Students should identify two of the following instances of figurative language: personification- "the little green leaves would not let me alone;" metaphor-the comparison of the smells of the sea to "a message of range and sweep/ Interwoven with waftures of wild-sea liberties;" metaphor-the gates of sleep
3. Answers will vary. **Possible answer:** The narrator of "Sunrise," even in his sleep, could smell the sea and the marshes. The air from the sea spoke to him of adventure and told of the large expanse that is the sea.
4. *Answers will vary.* **Possible answer:** Both poems describe the sunrise, and find a great amount of meaning in that time of the day. Both poems also describe nature as awesome, but at the same time people take part in and affect their natural surroundings. Lanier's poem "Sunrise" gives more readily understood details about how the narrator feels than does Porter's poem, which feels more ambiguous. "Sunrise" focuses more on a feeling of adventure than Porter's poem.
5. *Answers will vary.* Students should use effective figurative language at least three times.

11. Foreshadowing

1. *Answers will vary.* **Possible answer:** Blood is spilled during the French Revolution just like the red wine on the street. Many of the people who drank it, presumably some of the poor inhabitants of Paris, will be "stained" with blood like they were stained with wine.
2. During the French Revolution, "fools" who were "greedy" and "tigerish" held great sway over the people. In classic literature, the "fools" were often the ones who told the truth when others could not see it.
3. *Answers will vary.* **Possible answer:** Horatio is saying that, just as in ancient Rome, "heaven and earth," or the natural and supernatural, are joining together to foreshadow strange events.
4. *Answers will vary.* **Possible answer:** The audience would know immediately that something is wrong in the play, that the dead are dissatisfied enough to come back to warn the living of something. The atmosphere would be mysterious and dark.
5. *Answers will vary.* **Possible answer:** Foreshadowing can help authors keep their stories from feeling disjointed at times. If the beginning of *A Tale of Two Cities* didn't hint at violence, then that beginning, set before the Revolution actually starts, would feel like it belonged to a different book.

12. Imagery

1. *Answers will vary.* Reward genuine effort. **Possible answer:** Pound uses the word apparition to capture how the faces appeared to him suddenly, and struck him with an almost otherworldly beauty.
2. *Answers will vary.* **Possible answer:** The atmosphere is dreamlike.
3. **Answer:** Whitman appeals to: our sense of hearing ("When I heard the learn'd astronomer," "Look'd up in perfect silence at the stars"), and sight ("when the proofs, the figures were ranged in columns before me," "look'd up in perfect silence at the stars")
4. *Answers will vary.* Reward genuine effort. **Possible answer:** The atmosphere of this poem plays off of the contrast between the sterile lecture halls of the astronomer and the moist night air. The atmosphere of the first part of the poem, which describes all the proofs of the astronomer, sounds tiresome and monotonous. When Whitman "glides" out by himself, though, the atmosphere feels "mystical." Whitman's description of the astronomer's diagrams contributes very

directly to the tedious atmosphere. His extensive list of proofs, figures, charts and diagrams help us to visualize how the astronomer is swamped by his mathematics. He would literally be too busy looking at them to look at the stars. Whitman then describes the night simply but vividly; he mentions the stars and lets them speak for themselves.

5. *Answers will vary.* Reward genuine effort. **Possible answers:** Yes, this is imagery. The phrase "nothing shows in front of my eyes" still conjures an image of blackness before the narrator's eyes. No, this is not an example of imagery. The point of the poem is to make us imagine the absence of an image and the absence of any sound.

13. Inversion

1. "The Lord is a shepherd to me, Therefore I shall not want: He doth cause me to lie down In the folds of tender grass."
2. *Answers will vary.* **Possible answer:** The inverted psalm feels more lyrical (because of the rhyme). The non-inverted version sounds more straightforward than the other one does.
3. *Answers will vary.* **Possible answer:** It means that the clock strikes the hour—that's the loudest sound a clock makes.
4. *Answers will vary.* **Possible answer:** The inversion breaks the thought up, and so the reader has to wait for the conclusion, like someone staring at a clock has to wait for the minutes to pass before the clock strikes the hour.
5. *Answers will vary.* Reward genuine effort and accurate inversions.

14. Irony

1. *Answers will vary.* **Possible answer:** Appleman paints a picture of people who try to keep all natural elements out of their lives. They clean their houses with the zeal of a crusader, so they think they are tough.
2. *Answers will vary.* **Possible answer:** It sounds like these indoor people, when they "brave confusion," are trying to keep their lives orderly. Nature can be chaotic, unlike a clean house.
3. *Answers will vary.* **Possible answer:** Yes, it is important. The short, rhymed lines of "Arthur" remind the reader of an ironic take on a nursery rhyme.
4. *Answers will vary.* **Possible answer:** Perhaps the character Arthur is supposed to have an accent. The accent is also another element of the situational irony; it comes off as random, but it's funny.
5. *Answers will vary.* Reward genuine effort.

15. Metaphor

1. *Answers will vary.* Students should support their answers using the metaphors in the poem.
2. *Answers will vary.* **Possible answer:** "A riddle in nine syllables" is too long, so it's no longer funny. The narrator is pregnant.
3. *Answers will vary.* **Possible answers:** When Blake thinks that he sees "a world in a grain of sand," he imagines that the grain of sand could have complex features, too small for the human eye. That would make it like the wild flower, which has a great amount of complexity for something so small. Blake sees beauty in nature which extends to the smallest natural things. That beauty tells him something of what the whole world, heaven, infinity, and eternity are like.
4. *Answers will vary.* Reward genuine effort.
5. *Answers will vary.* Reward genuine effort. **Possible answer:** Metaphors help us to organize our thoughts, in that we see similarities between things and thus learn about the individual objects in that light. But metaphors do "disorder" things at the same time—the narrator of Plath's poem, in reality, is not a melon, a red fruit, or a loaf of bread. So metaphors make our thoughts more orderly by mixing up aspects of the world around us. They are both orderly and disorderly.

16. Meter

1. Answer: ˘ / ˘ / ˘ / ˘ / ˘ / ˘ /
     ˘ / ˘ / ˘ / ˘ / ˘ /
     ˘ / ˘ / ˘ / ˘ / ˘ /
     ˘ / ˘ / ˘ / ˘ / ˘ /
2. *Answers will vary.* **Possible answer:** The atmosphere is quiet, peaceful, and wistful.
3. Answer: ˘ / ˘ / ˘ / ˘ / ˘ /
     ˘ / / ˘ / ˘ / ˘ /
4. Iamb examples: report, content, trapeze, etc.; Trochee examples: pattern, region, lover, etc.
5. *Answers will vary.* Reward genuine effort.

17. Onomatopoeia

1. *Answers will vary.* **Possible answer:** The Atmosphere is one of merry and cheerful excitement.
2. *Answers will vary.* Students should demonstrate they have thought about the connection between the sounds of the

words and the atmosphere, or the mood of the poem. **<u>Possible answer:</u>** The onomatopoeias successfully create a feeling of merriment. The repetition of the T-sounds sounds a lot like sleigh bells.

3. *Answers will vary.* **<u>Possible answers</u>** include: Sammy feels that his job is monotonous. He's used the cash register so many times that it is accompanied by a predictable song he can't get out of his head. He is also sarcastic towards the customers, as shown when he calls them "hap-py pee-pul." Sammy may be bored with the routine of his job, but he has made it more enjoyable for himself by singing along to the sounds of the cash register.

4. *Answers will vary.* **<u>Possible answers:</u>** bam, achoo, chirp, crackle, hiss, murmur, etc.

5. *Answers will vary.* **<u>Possible answer:</u>** Onomatopoeias make prose and poetry feel more tangible than some other ordinary words would. When we read about a bird singing, we can see it in our minds. But if an onomatopoeia is used, we can also hear it singing in our minds. We can understand the subject of a poem more readily if we can use several senses to comprehend it.

18. Personification

1. *Answers will vary.* **<u>Possible answer:</u>** Sandburg portays Tomorrow as unfeeling, even if she may be right in saying "Let the dead be dead." Sandburg feels that the future marches on without a thought of the consequences and without any sentimental feelings about the past.

2. *Answers will vary.* **<u>Possible answer:</u>** The fly is like a child because Blake calls it "little fly," as if he were cooing at it. Blake also refers to its "summer's play."

3. *Answers will vary.* **<u>Possible answer:</u>** Blake is trying to remind us that, even though we all think our actions are important in the grand scheme of things, they might just be "play" that can be swatted away.

4. *Answers will vary.* Students should supply an example.

5. *Answers will vary.* Students should supply at least one reason.

19. Plot

1. *Answers will vary.* Answers should demonstrate understanding of conflict.

2. *Answers will vary.* Answers should demonstrate understanding of rising action.

3. *Answers will vary.* Answers should demonstrate understanding of climax.

4. *Answers will vary.* Answers should demonstrate understanding of falling action and resolution.

5. *Answers will vary.* **<u>Possible answer:</u>** A story needs conflict in order to be a story. A story without conflict would be uninteresting. Also, when there's conflict and tension in a story, it shows that the events in the story have a purpose and are geared toward a certain ending. Without conflict, the events wouldn't have much meaning.

20. Point of View

1. Answer: Buster Keaton

2. *Answers will vary.* **<u>Possible answer:</u>** Buster Keaton was a comedic actor who did a lot of physical comedy. Alberti's tone is a humorous one; he thinks that Keaton's antics are ridiculous.

3. Answer: The narrator knows what the Old Man "supposed," or thought. The narrator also knows enough about the Old Man to call him "futile."

4. *Answers will vary.* **<u>Possible answer:</u>** "The Village Burglar" lists only observable qualities about the burglar, which means that readers have to fill in the motives and moral judgments for themselves, unlike with "There was an Old Man Who Supposed."

5. *Answers will vary.* Reward genuine effort.

21. Refrain

1. *Answers will vary.* **<u>Possible answer:</u>** It is significant that the two words rhyme because it means they sound similar in the narrator's mind. It's as though if he heard "Lenore," he would hear echoes of "Nevermore," and vice versa.

2. *Answers will vary.* **<u>Possible answer:</u>** The narrator basically wants to be left alone, but the raven is especially intrusive, as the narrator realizes when he says, "Take thy beak from out my heart." The raven is not only disturbing the narrator's external solitude, but also his internal emotional state.

3. *Answers will vary.* **<u>Possible answer:</u>** For the narrator, the night doesn't feel whole, like it did when he and his lover were still together. The stars are far away from him, and instead of twinkling, they "shiver" in the cold. It's sad because even the night sky feels vulnerable and fragmented.

4. *Answers will vary.* **<u>Possible answer:</u>** The atmosphere is sad, and the narrator feels nostalgic for what he's lost.

5. *Answers will vary.* Reward genuine effort.

22. Rhyme

1. *Answers will vary.* **Possible answer:** End rhyme offers a sense of completeness of sound, as in Smith's "Sunt Leones." The internal rhyme in "The Walloping Window-Blind" quickens the pace of the poem, and gives it a galloping rhythm.
2. *Answers will vary.* **Possible answer:** The rhyme in "Sunt Leones" sounds traditional and creates a regular pace. The slant rhyme in "Greek Architecture" slows the poem down, whereas end rhymes lead you quickly to the next line.
3. *Answers will vary.* **Possible answer:** Disch writes incomplete lines to capture the feeling of reading a boring book, which drags on and on.
4. *Answers will vary.* **Possible answer:** The poem sounds humorous. One can also imagine a stuffy, proper man reading the poem, over-enunciating each word.
5. *Answers will vary.* Reward genuine effort.

23. Rhythm

1. *Answers will vary.* **Possible answer:** It suits the uncertainty. The rhythm of the second and third lines gives equal importance to the copper sun and scarlet sea, and the jungle star and jungle track. It's hard to pick which of these options is more likely to be an answer.
2. *Answers will vary.* **Possible answer:** No, it would not roll off the tongue so easily.
3. *Answers will vary.* **Possible answer:** Brooks ends each line with "We" so that we have to pause at the end. This adds a prolonged pause at the end of each line, which affects the rhythm.
4. *Answers will vary.* **Possible answer:** Brooks doesn't think that the boys are as cool as they think they are; it is a lament.
5. *Answers will vary.* Reward genuine effort.

24. Simile

1. *Answers will vary.* Students should list all four of the similes from "Harlem," choosing one to write on. The four similes: a dream deferred is "like a raisin in the sun," like a festering sore, like rotten meat that stinks, and like a sugared-over sweet. Reward genuine effort.
2. *Answers will vary.* **Possible answer:** "Harlem" is about what happens when people don't act on their dreams, either because of procrastination or because their circumstances prevent them from acting. The dreams stay within them and basically turn sour. They turn into disappointment, and sometimes "explode" into rage.
3. *Answers will vary.* Reward genuine effort. **Possible answer:** The "white radiance of Eternity" is a simple light, only made up of one color. When people perceive that radiance, they have to see it through a mortal perspective. We take the simple and eternal white radiance and confuse it in our limited minds, breaking it into little pieces. But the end result of this confusion is beautiful, like a stained-glass window.
4. *Answers will vary.* Reward genuine effort.
5. *Answers will vary.* Reward genuine effort. **Possible answer:** The simile from Hughes' poem, "does [a dream deferred] dry up/like a raisin in the sun?" is a compelling simile. One can easily imagine a dream losing all of its vitality and healthfulness. It shrivels up and shrinks up with age. A good simile, like the example from "Harlem," compares two things that are actually strikingly similar, even though they seem to be completely different. The apt comparison made by the simile comes as a sort of surprise to the imagination, causing it to have an "a-ha!" moment. It recognizes that the simile makes a shrewd comparison.

25. Sonnet

1. *Answers will vary.* **Possible answer:** When the narrator sees everything around him age and decay, he has to wonder if his beloved will stay beautiful as the years pass. The only thing that can be done about this universal decay is to have children, in order to see yourself young again in the form of your child.
2. *Answers will vary.* **Possible answer:** Yes, it is songlike because of the rhyme scheme. Also, it's confessional and wistful, which make it a good candidate for a song.
3. *Answers will vary.* **Possible answer:** No, because children grow old, too.
4. *Answers will vary.* **Possible answer:** Earlier in the sonnet, Patience tells Milton that "who best/bear his mild yoke, they serve him best." So those who "stand and wait" are serving God by waiting to listen to him, and not trying to serve in their own way.
5. *Answers will vary.* Reward genuine effort.

26. Style

1. *Answers will vary.* **Possible answer:** The atmosphere feels mysterious because of the fragmented thoughts.
2. *Answers will vary.* **Possible answer:** One can hear someone reading the poem, breaking off every time there's a dash as though he or she were hesitating.
3. *Answers will vary.* **Possible answer:** This passage is very reserved, and the raised voice that comes with a question mark would be too strong of a display of emotion.
4. *Answers will vary.* **Possible answer:** Cummings and Dickinson both have a unique style. They both use the visual format of their poem to communicate their meaning—Dickinson with her dashes and Cummings with his isolated letters. Among these two poems at least, Cummings use of words might be more unconventional than Dickinson's.
5. *Answers will vary.* Reward genuine effort.

27. Symbolism

1. *Answers will vary.* **Possible answer:** Cooking everything separately represents a cleaner approach to life. It attempts to exert too much control over what happens, instead of just letting things blend together.
2. *Answers will vary.* Reward genuine effort. **Possible answer:** The blackbird symbolizes "a small part of the pantomime," or the power of nature to speak to us without words.
3. *Answers will vary.* Some other examples include: birds standing for freedom, chains standing for imprisonment, sunlight standing for clarity.
4. *Answers will vary.* Reward genuine effort. **Possible answer:** Many symbols are unique to certain cultures. However, the commonality of the human experience has yielded universal symbols as well.
5. *Answers will vary.* Reward genuine effort. **Possible answer:** Yeats thinks that poetry shouldn't *tell* it readers about truth; it should *show* them truth using symbols. The imagination only desires "to gaze upon some reality, some beauty." Yeats speaks of a reality that is too complicated to be summed up with moral maxims. Symbols can deal more effectively with complexity than can abstract ideas. Creative writing is more effective when it uses symbolism and other figurative language. Readers of poetry and fiction usually don't want to be told explicitly what to think about a certain issue. Symbolism is more suggestive, because it can give hints of many different answers to a certain question, without necessarily favoring one of those answers.

28. Theme

1. *Answers will vary.* **Possible answer:** The theme of this excerpt is that people are inextricably related to each other. Even on a spiritual level, a person can't stand alone.
2. *Answers will vary.* Reward genuine effort. **Possible answer:** The language of the excerpt does support the theme. Steinbeck captures the regional dialect of a certain population group in America. By letting Tom Joad speak in this way, Steinbeck is showing respect for all kinds of people, no matter how they speak, thus recognizing that everyone deserves to be part of a "great soul."
3. *Answers will vary.* Reward genuine effort. Students should support their answers.
4. *Answers will vary.* **Possible answer:** These images really show just how things changed when "the conquerors came." Things seemed completely opposite to the Mayans, not just slightly different.
5. *Answers will vary.* Reward genuine effort.

29. Tone

1. *Answers will vary.* **Possible answer:** A machine's "life" consists of its being used. So a machine that's lying in the grass has no more life to it.
2. *Answers will vary.* **Possible answer:** Conrad's tone is one of disgust towards the incompetence encountered by Marlow.
3. *Answers will vary.* **Possible answer:** This image shows that war is not only not kind, but also something outside of our everyday, "civilized" existence. The lover's "wild" manner of death shows that that he is asking heaven, or the "sky," why he is dying.
4. *Answers will vary.* **Possible answer:** Yes, Crane is being ironic. There's no way war could be kind when the maiden's lover died feeling powerless and alone. According to Crane, no honor lauded by war could make up for this kind of death.
5. *Answers will vary.* **Possible answer:** "I saw an unused boiler in the grass, then found a path leading up the hill." If the sentence were written this way, the reader might still wonder why the boiler was unused. With the absence of an emotionally charged word like "wallowing," though, it wouldn't seem like anything was wrong with the boiler not being in use.

1. ALLEGORY

*A story in which characters, actions,
or settings represent abstract ideas*

Symbolism comes to life in an allegory. Allegories are fictional tales where characters, their actions, and the story's setting symbolize an abstract idea. These characters breathe life into the ideas they represent.

Dante's *Divine Comedy* is a lengthy, complex allegory. Vivid in its **imagery** and memorable in its language, Dante's poem describes an imaginary journey through hell, purgatory, and finally through heaven. This journey is an allegory of Dante's search for salvation and the obstacles he has to surmount before he can achieve his goal.

> *"Midway upon the journey of our life*
> *I found myself within a forest dark,*
> *For the straightforward pathway had been lost.*
> *Ah me! how hard a thing it is to say*
> *What was this forest savage, rough, and stern,*
> *Which in the very thought renews the fear."*
>
> —from *The Inferno,* by Dante Alighieri

In this passage, Dante describes how he found himself lost in a dark forest. It soon becomes clear, however, that this dark forest isn't really a place, but a state of mind in which "the straightforward pathway had been lost."

Allegories and *parables,* which are allegories used to teach morals, are often religious. The New Testament, for example, is filled with parables which help relate heavenly concepts to life on earth.

Allegories and parables are not limited to religious topics. In his imaginative autobiography *Bound for Glory,* folksinger Woody Guthrie writes about a tornado, which he calls "Mister Cyclone," that ripped through his hometown when he was a young boy. The young Woody and his father fight for their lives, trying to reach a storm shelter. When they finally get there, Guthrie says:

> *"And I drifted off to sleep thinking about all of the people in the world that have worked*
> *hard and had somebody else come along and take their life away from them."*

Guthrie goes through a long description of the tornado as a force of nature that destroys people's houses and farms. Then, in the above passage, it's finally clear that the tornado represents more than a tornado, and that the story is an allegory. Like Dante's *Divine Comedy,* it's a vivid story, the lessons of which stay with us long after we finish reading.

❶ *ANALYZE*   If the "straightforward pathway" represents the path toward God for Dante, then what does the "dark" forest represent?

_____

_____

❷ *EXPLAIN*   As the passage from *The Inferno* continues, Dante describes how he found himself in the dark woods:

> *"I cannot well repeat how there I entered,*
> *So full was I of slumber at the moment*
> *In which I had abandoned the true way."*

What do you think this means?

_____

_____

_____

❸ *IN YOUR OWN WORDS*   What does the tornado symbolize in the excerpt from *Bound for Glory*?

_____

_____

_____

❹ *EVALUATE*   Do you think the tornado is a fitting symbol in this work?

_____

_____

_____

5 Why might writers choose to write allegorically, instead of just saying what they mean directly? Write as much or as little as you need to. You do not have to use this entire page, and you can use additional sheets if necessary.

_____

_____

_____

_____

_____

_____

_____

_____

_____

_____

_____

_____

_____

_____

_____

_____

_____

_____

_____

_____

2. ALLITERATION

When two or more words begin with the
same sound, usually a consonant

Even before we understand the meaning of words, we hear the sounds. Dylan Thomas recounts what it was like each time he heard a word for the first time as a young child. These words were "as the notes of bells, the sounds of musical instruments, the noises of wind, sea, and rain, the rattle of milk-carts…the fingering of branches on a window pane…might be to someone, deaf from birth, who has miraculously found his hearing." Thomas recognized early on the importance of sounds in literature.

There are many literary elements that reflect how poetry and prose utilize the sound of words; one of these is alliteration. Alliteration is often used to draw attention to something, as in this poem about Isaac Newton:

> *"Nature and Nature's laws lay hid in night.*
> *God said, Let Newton be! And all was light."*
>
> > —from "Epitaph, Intended for Sir Isaac Newton in Westminster Abbey,"
> > by Alexander Pope

Pope begins several words in the poem with the letter N and others with the letter L; in the first line, he creates tension as we wait for what is hidden to be revealed. Then Newton comes along, and "all was light."

William Shakespeare also uses alliteration in the play *Macbeth*.

> *"To-morrow, and to-morrow, and to-morrow,*
> *Creeps in this petty pace from day to day,*
> *To the last syllable of recorded time;*
> *And all our yesterdays have lighted fools*
> *The way to dusty death. Out, out, brief candle!*
> *Life's but a walking shadow, a poor player,*
> *That struts and frets his hour upon the stage,*
> *And then is heard no more. It is a tale*
> *Told by an idiot, full of sound and fury,*
> *Signifying nothing."*

There are many instances of alliteration in this speech, including the repetition of the T-sound in the first line and the D-sound in the second. The plodding repetition of these words imitates the "petty pace" of days marching on. Shakespeare even hints at the power of sound in the third line, where days "creep" to "the last syllable of recorded time." The sound of words can enhance our reading experience or the actual meaning of the literary work. Whenever we hear and see words in a new context, it's almost as if we are struck by them anew, like a deaf person who can suddenly hear (as Thomas wrote).

Understanding ALLITERATION

❶ UNDERSTAND Why does Alexander Pope claim that "Nature and Nature's laws lay hid in night" before Newton?

_____

_____

_____

_____

_____

_____

❷ HEARING IT ALOUD Read Pope's "Epitaph" for Newton aloud. Does this enhance the alliteration? Explain.

_____

_____

_____

_____

_____

❸ EXAMPLE Provide an example of alliteration from a popular song or other work.

_____

_____

_____

❹ MEMORIZE Memorize the famous passage from William Shakespeare's _Macbeth_. Recite it for your class or for a small group of classmates.

Writing with ALLITERATION

❺ In the soliloquy from *Macbeth,* Macbeth discusses the passage of time and what he thinks of life. Write a paragraph or short poem addressing one or both of these subjects, using alliteration at least three times. Write as much or as little as you need to. You do not have to use this entire page, and you can use additional sheets if necessary.

3. ALLUSION

*A reference to a well-known person, place,
or thing in history or in fiction*

One thing often reminds us of another. A random object or event can trigger the memory of something that happened years ago; when this happens, your present situation feels connected to your past experience. Writers try to recreate this feeling when they use allusions. An allusion in a novel can remind us of a song we've heard, which in turn brings a newspaper article to mind. Allusions come in many shapes and sizes. Allusions can be direct or indirect.

Stephen Daedalus, a character in the novel *Ulysses,* uses a few *direct illusions* in a conversation with his friends.

> *"Maeterlinck says: If Socrates leave his house today he will find the sage seated on his doorstep. If Judas go forth tonight it is to Judas his steps will tend."*

> —from *Ulysses,* by James Joyce

In this passage, Stephen appeals to authority, a French writer named Maurice Maeterlinck, to justify his opinion; Stephen believes that you're always basically the same person, no matter where you go or what you do.

At the same time, Joyce reminds his readers of other ideas in history. His allusions put thoughts of Socrates the philosopher, the "sage," and Judas the betrayer in our minds as we continue to read *Ulysses.*

An *indirect allusion* does not explicitly state that to which it refers. Edna St. Vincent Millay refers indirectly to the New Testament in her two-line poem "Second Fig."

> *"Safe upon the solid rock the ugly houses stand:*
> *Come and see my shining palace built upon the sand!"*

This poem humorously changes the words of Matthew. Readers have most likely heard the original version of this phrase—"Therefore everyone who hears these words of mine and puts them into practice is like a wise man who built his house on the rock . . . . But everyone who hears these words of mine and does not put them into practice is like a foolish man who built his house on sand" (Matthew 7:24-27). Readers will know that the poem differs in meaning from the biblical passage.

When we write, we draw on all parts of our experience, which include the things we've read and heard about as well as what we see every day. Allusions can broaden the meaning of a writer's work, allowing the author to take advantage of a long history of shared knowledge, culture, and tradition.

❶ **EXPLAIN** What do you think is meant by Stephen's quote from Maeterlinck, *"If Socrates leave his house today he will find the sage seated on his doorstep. If Judas go forth tonight it is to Judas his steps will tend"*? Do you agree with the explanation given? Explain.

_____

_____

_____

_____

❷ **RESEARCH** Stephen Daedalus's last name is a direct allusion to an ancient Greek inventor, Daedalus. Research the life of Daedalus. What might this allusion show about Stephen, who is a poet?

_____

_____

_____

❸ **ANALYZE** How would you interpret the meaning of "Second Fig"?

_____

_____

_____

❹ **COMPARE/CONTRAST** Do you think that direct and indirect allusions could affect readers differently? Use the passage from *Ulysses* and "Second Fig" to support your answer.

_____

_____

_____

_____

Using ALLUSIONS

❺ Think of a childhood experience that stands out in your mind. Write a paragraph about that experience using at least three allusions, either direct or indirect (at least one of each). Write as much or as little as you need to. You do not have to use this entire page, and you can use additional sheets if necessary.

4. ANALOGY

An analogy compares two things closely

You've probably heard the objection, "That's like comparing apples to oranges," when someone compares two very different kinds of things. The truth is, though, that apples and oranges are just as similar as they are different. Analogies in literature often compare things that seem to differ in kind, but which turn out to have many things in common, like apples and oranges. By pointing out both these differences and similarities, analogies offer a new perspective on each object.

Craig Raine's poem, "A Martian Sends a Postcard Home," is written from the **point of view** of a Martian who uses analogies to explain what earth is like to his friends and family on Mars.

> *"Model T is a room with the lock inside—*
> *a key is turned to free the world*
>
> *for movement, so quick there is a film*
> *to watch for anything missed."*

The Martian's audience has probably never seen a car before, so the Martian compares the inside of a car to a room with a lock inside. Once you unlock it, you "free the world for movement." By showing how a car could be strange and astonishing to a Martian, Raine implies that a car should also seem extraordinary, and not mundane, to people.

In "What is it to be Human?" Waldo Williams uses analogies to establish a kind of equality between concepts and images.

> *"What is staying alive? To possess*
> *A great hall inside of a cell."*

When we think of what it means to stay alive, we think of things like food, water, and shelter. But Williams asks us to look inward at the tiny cells that constitute our bodies, calling them "great halls." Similarly, Williams sees knowledge in an unconventional way. He asks:

> *"What is to know? The same root*
> *underneath the branches."*

Learning is not just the collection of facts, but also the act of connecting ideas.

In both of these poems, Raine and Williams create analogies between seemingly different things to change the way we think about them. Apples and oranges are not so different after all, and neither are Model Ts and moving rooms.

Understanding ANALOGY

❶ DESCRIBE How would you describe a Model T, or a modern car, to someone who had never seen one before (whether extraterrestrial or not)? What analogies would you use to help him or her understand?

_____

_____

_____

❷ ANALYZE How do you think the Martian feels about the freedom of movement generated by a car? Have you ever felt this way before?

_____

_____

_____

❸ EXPLAIN In "What is it to be Human," why do you think Williams equates "staying alive" to possessing "a great hall inside of a cell," and the act of knowing to "the same root underneath the branches?" Do these analogies make sense?

_____

_____

_____

_____

❹ COMPARE/CONTRAST Compare the analogy from Raine's poem and one of the analogies from Williams' poem. How are these two analogies different? How are they alike? Which one do you like better? Why?

_____

_____

_____

_____

5 Think about three things you encounter every day—traffic lights, school hallways, your backyard, etc.—and create three analogies that describe them.

_____

_____

_____

_____

_____

_____

_____

_____

_____

_____

_____

_____

_____

_____

_____

_____

_____

_____

_____

_____

_____

_____

_____

_____

_____

_____

5. ASSONANCE

The repetition of vowel sounds in two or more words that appear close to each other, while not repeating the surrounding consonants

Do not only mind your p's and q's, but also your a's, e's, i's, o's, u's, and sometimes y's. Assonance, like **alliteration,** uses a repetition of similar sounds to create a certain effect. **Alliteration** is a repetition of similar consonant sounds, but assonance is a repetition of similar vowel sounds. These two elements show just how important sound is in literature.

In the following poem, assonance helps Lord Byron paint a portrait of a beautiful woman.

> *"And on that cheek, and o'er that brow,*
> *So soft, so calm, yet eloquent,*
> *The smiles that win, the tints that glow,*
> *But tell of days in goodness spent,*
> *A mind at peace with all below,*
> *A heart whose love is innocent!"*

> —from "She Walks in Beauty," by George Gordon, Lord Byron

The words "win" and "tint," "glow" and "below," and "spent, innocent" all use similar vowel sounds. (Note: although there is rhyming here, it is not a part of the assonance.) **Alliteration** can sometimes sound harsh as it rolls off the tongue. Assonance creates a slightly softer effect, and the words blend together. When a poet uses assonance, he or she is using this blending effect to their advantage, connecting words and ideas together in the reader's mind.

Lord Tennyson uses sound very effectively in the following poem, "The Splendor Falls on Castle Walls."

> *"The splendor falls on castle walls*
> *And snowy summits old in story;*
> *The long light shakes across the lakes,*
> *And the wild cataract leaps in glory.*
> *Blow, bugle, blow, set the wild echoes flying,*
> *Blow, bugle; answer, echoes dying, dying, dying."*

Assonance shows up several times—"falls" and "walls," and "shakes" and "lakes." (Again the rhyming is incidental.) Because our attention is drawn to these otherwise ordinary words, we slow down and concentrate on the images they create.

By directing our attention to certain sounds, Byron and Tennyson make us focus on each line of the poem. At the same time, they show how the written word can be musical. Assonance is just one of the many ways to make us tune in more closely to literature.

Understanding ASSONANCE

❶ HEARING IT ALOUD Read the excerpt from "She Walks in Beauty" aloud. In general, how does it sound?

_____

_____

❷ ANALYZE Why do you think Lord Byron uses assonance? What effect does it have on you?

_____

_____

_____

_____

❸ MEMORIZE Memorize the verse from "The Splendor Falls on Castle Walls," and recite it for you class or a group of classmates. Pay attention to the instances of assonance.

❹ COMPARE/CONTRAST In the second line of "The Splendor Falls on Castle Walls," Tennyson uses **alliteration** in the phrase "snowy summits." Read this phrase aloud. Do you think it affects the reader differently than assonance does (for example, "falls" and "walls")? How so? Which do you prefer?

_____

_____

_____

_____

_____

_____

_____

_____

Writing with ASSONANCE

5 Write a descriptive paragraph or short poem about a place you like in nature. Use assonance at least three times. Write as much or as little as you need to. You do not have to use this entire page, and you can use additional sheets if necessary.

_____

_____

_____

_____

_____

_____

_____

_____

_____

_____

_____

_____

_____

_____

_____

_____

_____

_____

_____

_____

_____

6. ATMOSPHERE

The mood or feelings brought forth by a poem or a piece of prose

When you write, it's important to "set the scene." The mood of a passage should jump off the page. Writers provide lots of sensory details so that "readers" can imagine being *in* the book, and they describe characters, events, and settings so that, all together, they give off a certain feeling.

The atmosphere of a piece of writing can be eerie, cheerful, contemplative, etc. The possibilities are endless.

Elizabeth Alexander's poem, "Praise Song for the Day," has an atmosphere of hopeful anticipation.

> *"A woman and her son wait for the bus.*
> *A farmer considers the changing sky.*
> *A teacher says,* Take out your pencils. Begin."

All of the characters here are waiting to see what will happen next, but they still are about to take action. The woman and her son will climb aboard the bus, the farmer will make decisions about the weather, and students, pencils poised, will take a test or write an essay. None of the characters can be sure of the outcome, but that doesn't stop them. It's no surprise when, later in the poem, Alexander writes:

> *"I know there's something better down the road…*
> *We walk into that which we cannot yet see."*

The atmosphere of the following passage from Irene Nemirovsky's *Suite Française* differs from that of "Praise Song for the Day," but it is just as compelling.

> *"Hot, thought the Parisians. The warm air of spring. It was night, they were at war and there was an air raid. But dawn was near and the war far away. The first to hear the hum of the siren were those who couldn't sleep…. To them it began as a long breath, like air being forced into a deep sigh. It wasn't long before its wailing filled the sky. It came from afar, from beyond the horizon, slowly, almost lazily. Those still asleep dreamed of waves breaking over pebbles, a March storm whipping the woods… until finally sleep was shaken off and they struggled to open their eyes, murmuring, 'Is it an air raid?'"*

The passage takes place during World War II, right before the German invasion of Paris. Nemirovsky creates a dreamlike, languid atmosphere, which may seem strange for a wartime setting. Yet this passage helps us place ourselves in the shoes of ordinary people who wake up to an extraordinary reality. Nemirovsky ensures that the reader can feel the hot Parisian air and that he or she hears the wail of the siren. As with Alexander's poem, readers feel involved in this passage, and can sense what it would be like to be there.

Understanding ATMOSPHERE

❶ DESCRIBE How would you describe the atmosphere of Alexander's "Praise Song for the Day?"

_____

_____

_____

_____

❷ ANALYZE How do the images used in "Praise Song for the Day" help to create the atmosphere?

_____

_____

_____

_____

❸ MAKE A LIST List three of the details in the passage from _Suite Française_ that "set the scene" for the reader.

_____

_____

_____

❹ YOU DECIDE The passage from _Suite Française_ takes place in a city about to be invaded. Given this fact, do you think that the atmosphere of the passage makes sense?

_____

_____

_____

_____

_____

5 Think about a piece of writing which has an atmosphere that affected you. Your example can be from a novel, poem, short story, newspaper, or magazine. Describe its atmosphere and say why and how it affected you. Write as much or as little as you need to. You do not have to use this entire page, and you can use additional sheets if necessary.

_____

_____

_____

_____

_____

_____

_____

_____

_____

_____

_____

_____

_____

_____

_____

_____

_____

_____

_____

_____

7. BALLAD

A ballad is a short song or poem that tells a story

Herodotus, the great Greek historian, wrote so that "time may not draw the color from what man has brought into being." Ballads, which are usually dramatic tales, have been composed and sung for centuries. People who sang ballads were often illiterate, but this did not keep them from accessing an extensive tradition of storytelling.

A *folk ballad* is passed down orally and often has an unknown author. "The Bitter Withy," by an unknown writer, tells an unconventional tale about Jesus.

> *"As it fell out on a holy day,*
> *The drops of rain did fall, did fall,*
> *Our Savior asked leave of his mother Mary*
> *If he might go play ball.*
>
> *'To play at ball, my own dear son,*
> *It's time you was going or gone,*
> *But be sure let me hear no complain of you,*
> *At night when you do come home…'"*

This ballad is humorous and down-to-earth. It turns Jesus and Mary into normal people, people who themselves might sing ballads.

An *art ballad* is a modern poem that emulates a folk ballad, like "The Rime of the Ancient Mariner" by Samuel Taylor Coleridge.

> *"Water, water, everywhere,*
> *And all the boards did shrink;*
> *Water, water, everywhere,*
> *Nor any drop to drink.*
>
> *The very deep did rot: O Christ!*
> *That ever this should be!*
> *Yea, slimy things did crawl with legs*
> *Upon the slimy sea."*

Coleridge's poem imitates the **meter** of many folk ballads, where lines alternate between being eight syllables long and six syllables long ("every" in "everywhere" should be read as three syllables). The overall effect is very songlike.

Whether sung or written by an educated poet like Coleridge, ballads use poetry and music to tell stories. Like the writings of Herodotus, ballads preserve the "color" of human efforts and attitudes, from the past and present.

Understanding BALLADS

❶ EXPLAIN Why is the phrase "did fall" repeated in the second line of "The Bitter Withy"?

_____

_____

❷ YOU DECIDE Art ballads are written and are not passed down through song. Do you think "The Rime of the Ancient Mariner" could be easily sung?

_____

_____

❸ COMPARE/CONTRAST Compare the **atmosphere,** or overall feeling, of "The Rime of the Ancient Mariner" to that of "The Bitter Withy."

_____

_____

_____

_____

❹ DISCUSS Read "An Eastern Ballad" by Allen Ginsberg, an American poet. Most ballads are plot-driven tales, but "An Eastern Ballad" is more meditative. Why might Ginsberg have called this poem a ballad?

> "I speak of love that comes to mind:
> The moon is faithful, although blind;
> She moves in thought she cannot speak.
> Perfect care has made her bleak.
>
> I never dreamed the sea so deep,
> The earth so dark; so long my sleep,
> I have become another child.
> I wake to see the world go wild."

_____

_____

_____

5 Samuel Taylor Coleridge was only one of many poets to write art ballads, or literary ballads. What do you think motivates poets to try to emulate folk ballads? Write as much or as little as you need to. You do not have to use this entire page, and you can use additional sheets if necessary.

_____

_____

_____

_____

_____

_____

_____

_____

_____

_____

_____

_____

_____

_____

_____

_____

_____

_____

_____

_____

_____

_____

_____

8. CHARACTERIZATION

*All of the elements that come together to create
an imaginary person or character*

People are complex in real life, and a well-written character is too. As we become acquainted with characters in literature, we observe how they act and what they look like. We hear what they say, listen in to their thoughts, and eavesdrop as other characters think or talk about them.

In her story "A Good Man is Hard to Find," Flannery O'Connor creates a humorous, detailed snapshot of a character known simply as "the grandmother." The grandmother is about to embark on a road trip with her family. She "had her big black valise that looked like the head of a hippopotamus," and was ready to go. O'Connor continues:

> *"The old lady settled herself comfortably, removing her white cotton gloves and putting them up with her purse...the grandmother had on a navy blue straw sailor hat with a bunch of white violets on the brim and a navy blue dress with a small white dot in the print...In case of an accident, anyone seeing her dead on the highway would know at once that she was a lady."*

In *War and Peace,* Leo Tolstoy, a master of characterization, uses a similar wealth of details to describe Prince Bolkonsky. Tolstoy describes the old Russian nobleman's eccentric opinions.

> *"He used to say that there were only two sources of human vice: idleness and superstition; and that there were only two virtues: activity and intelligence."*

Tolstoy then shows us how other characters in his novel feel about Prince Bolkonsky.

> *"With the people around him, from his daughter to the servants, the prince was brusque and invariably demanding, and thus, without being cruel, inspired a fear and respect for himself such as the cruelest of men would not find it easy to obtain...each person in the waiting room experienced the same feeling of respect and even fear at the moment when the immensely high door to the study opened and revealed the small figure of the old man, in a powdered wig, with small dry hands and gray beetling brows, which sometimes, when he frowned, hid the brightness of his intelligent and youthfully bright eyes."*

The portraits O'Connor and Tolstoy painted of their characters are multifaceted and tangible enough to be real. We could even expect to run into these characters on the street someday.

❶ **BREAK IT DOWN**   Refer to the list of techniques for characterization given in the first paragraph of the previous page. Identify the techniques O'Connor uses to describe the grandmother.

_____

_____

_____

_____

❷ **ANALYZE**   What kind of **tone,** or attitude, does the narrator of "A Good Man is Hard to Find," take towards the grandmother?

_____

_____

_____

❸ **INFER**   As the story continues, the grandmother changes. In other words, she is a _dynamic_ character. Would you expect that outcome, given the description of her on the previous page? Why or why not?

_____

_____

_____

_____

❹ **EXAMINE**   Reread the end of the excerpt from _War and Peace._ Did the description of Prince Bolkonsky's entrance into the Great Hall surprise you? If so, why?

_____

_____

_____

_____

Creating a CHARACTER

❺ Think about someone you know who is interesting and unique, or create your own fictional character. Write a paragraph describing that person, giving him or her a few different qualities. Write as much or as little as you need to. You do not have to use this entire page, and you can use additional sheets if necessary.

_____

_____

_____

_____

_____

_____

_____

_____

_____

_____

_____

_____

_____

_____

_____

_____

_____

_____

_____

_____

_____

_____

9. COUPLET

A couplet is two lines, generally written in the same style

A lot can be said in two lines of poetry. A couplet is made of two lines which, in some way, relate to each other. They usually **rhyme** with each other and are written with the same **meter.** Couplets also usually make up one complete thought.

John Denham's poem "The Thames" consists entirely of couplets. The following lines are in *iambic pentameter* and follow an *a a b b* **rhyme** scheme.

> *"O, could I flow like thee, and make thy stream*
> *My great example, as it is my theme!*
> *Though deep, yet clear, though gentle, yet not dull;*
> *Strong without rage, without o'erflowing full."*

In the first couplet, the narrator talks about how he wishes to learn from the river. The second couplet then describes the river, letting us know why the narrator would want to learn from it. The two couplets are related in content, but they each present two different thoughts. After reading the first couplet, satisfied with its symmetry and **rhyme,** we are able to take a breath. We then are ready for the next couplet and the next thought.

Couplets work well together, but they also pack enough punch to stand on their own. The following poem consists of only one couplet.

> *"I who by day am function of the light*
> *Am constant and invariant by night."*

> —from "Motto for a Sun Dial," by J.V. Cunningham

This poem gets a lot done in just two lines. It gives us satisfaction through the completed **rhyme** of "light" and "night." The **personification** of the sun dial is intriguing. The poem is emotionally suggestive, hinting that it's about more than just a sun dial. We learn that by day, a sun dial is like the dependent variable of a mathematical equation; its movement is dependent on sunlight. At night however, it's unchanging.

In many poems, couplets help us to jump from thought to thought, and they help a poem stay organized. A couplet is one of the basic units of poetry, but it can be more than just a unit, as Cunningham shows. It can stand as a poem on its own.

Understanding COUPLET

❶ EXPLAIN In John Denham's poem "The Thames," the narrator hopes that the river will be his "great example." How does a river serve as an example for someone? What can we learn from a river?

_____

_____

_____

_____

❷ ANALYZE Denham describes the Thames as being "deep, yet clear." What would a person be like if they were "deep, yet clear"?

_____

_____

_____

❸ ELEMENTAL CONNECTION Why do you think that J.V. Cunningham's "Motto for a Sun Dial" makes **allusions,** or references, to mathematics?

_____

_____

_____

_____

❹ IN YOUR OWN WORDS How would you interpret "Motto for a Sun Dial"?

_____

_____

_____

_____

_____

Writing COUPLETS

5 Make a poem out of a couplet. Write one couplet that would suffice for a poem; it can **rhyme** or not rhyme. Then try to write several more.

10. FIGURATIVE LANGUAGE

*Any use of language not meant to be taken literally,
such as similes, metaphors, and personification*

Life, for all of its twists and turns, would be pretty boring without figurative language. Many situations call for speaking literally, and often there is a need for literal language in the most creative of poems. Yet if we were limited to "just the facts" of life, the world around us would end with what we could see and touch. There wouldn't be much room for the imagination, which helps us see beyond our daily experiences.

Anne Porter uses figurative language to describe the sunrise.

> *"At six o'clock this morning*
> *I saw the rising sun*
> *Resting on the ground like a boulder…*
> *A single great ember*
> *About the height of a man."*

—from "Four Poems in One," by Anne Porter

There are few facts in this poem, but it's still an accurate description of a sunrise. Porter uses a **simile** when she says she saw the low sun "resting on the ground like a boulder," and a **metaphor** when she calls the sun "a single great ember." We are not supposed to think that the sun actually stands "about the height of a man" in comparison to us, but this line expresses how close we can feel to the sun at dawn.

Sydney Lanier, in a poem called "Sunrise," also describes the early morning with figurative language.

> *"The little green leaves would not let me alone in my sleep;*
> *Up-breathed from the marshes, a message of range and of sweep*
> *Interwoven with waftures of wild sea-liberties, drifting,*
> *Came through the lapped leaves sifting, sifting,*
> *Came to the gates of sleep."*

This poem would be quite different if the narrator simply said he was awoken by the smell of air coming from the sea. His language goes beyond what actually happened, letting us feel as the narrator did that morning. He felt "wild sea-liberties" in the air, and we, with him, are tempted to leap out of bed and run to the marshes. Lanier would not have been able to share this sense of adventure so effectively without figurative language.

As we look out at our physical environment, we can't help but let our imagination influence the way we perceive it. Figurative language results from this blending of the imagination and reality.

❶ *ANALYZE* Anne Porter describes the sun as though it is "resting on the ground like a bolder." Why does she portray the sun in this way?

_____

_____

_____

❷ *IDENTIFY* There are several instances of figurative language in "Sunrise," including **personification** and **metaphor.** Identify two of these instances.

_____

_____

_____

❸ *IN YOUR OWN WORDS* Paraphrase the poem "Sunrise."

_____

_____

_____

❹ *COMPARE/CONTRAST* The excerpts from "Four Poems in One" and "Sunrise" both take place at sunrise. How do the two poems differ, and how are they alike?

_____

_____

_____

_____

5 Think about a time when you saw the sun rise. Write a paragraph describing that time, using figurative language at least three times. Write as much or as little as you need to. You do not have to use this entire page, and you can use additional sheets if necessary.

_____

_____

_____

_____

_____

_____

_____

_____

_____

_____

_____

_____

_____

_____

_____

_____

_____

_____

_____

_____

_____

_____

_____

_____

_____

11. FORESHADOWING

An indication of events to come

In literature, it is sometimes possible to tell the future. You don't need a crystal ball, though, to determine what will happen next. Instead, many authors leave clues about how their story or poem will end, and what will happen in the meantime. These hints make a story feel cohesive. Foreshadowing also intrigues readers and keeps them reading, eager to find out what happens at the end.

At the beginning of *A Tale of Two Cities* by Charles Dickens, a cask of red wine falls off of a wagon and breaks in the street. Men and women run to drink the wine. This event foreshadows the French Revolution.

> *"The wine was red wine, and had stained the ground of the narrow street.... It had stained many hands, too, and many faces, and many naked feet, and many wooden shoes…Those who had been greedy with the staves of the cask, had acquired a tigerish smear about the mouth; and one tall joker so besmirched… scrawled upon a wall with his finger dipped in muddy wine-lees [wine sediment]—blood.*
>
> *The time was to come, when that wine too would be spilled on the street-stones, and when the stain of it would be red upon many there."*

Dickens' intent is unmistakable. Readers know to expect violence and ferocity, especially from those who wear "a tigerish smear" on their faces.

One of William Shakespeare's most famous plays, *Hamlet, Prince of Denmark,* hardly has a chance to begin before a ghost of Hamlet's father appears. Hamlet's friend, Horatio, compares the appearance of the ghost to the omens, or "fierce events," that foreshadowed the death of Julius Caesar.

> *"And even the like presence of fierce events,*
> *As harbingers preceding still the fates*
> *And prologue to the omen coming on,*
> *Have heaven and earth together demonstrated*
> *Unto our climatures and countrymen."*

Readers of Shakespeare's play do not quite know what to expect, but the play's gloomy and mysterious beginning cannot bode well. It is no surprise that the play ends with the death of many of the characters, and on the way includes insanity, betrayal, and suicide.

If you've ever finished a book, returned to the beginning, and realized that the ending was practically written in the first paragraph of the first chapter, it's because that author used foreshadowing. Good writers choose every single word for a reason, and foreshadowing is just one of the ways they show they have the whole story in mind as they write.

❶ EXPLAIN Explain in your own words how the excerpt from *A Tale of Two Cities* foreshadows violence.

_____

_____

_____

_____

❷ INFER Why does Dickens have a "joker," instead of another, more serious kind of character, write "blood" on the wall?

_____

_____

_____

_____

❸ IN YOUR OWN WORDS Paraphrase the passage from *Hamlet.* Look up any words you don't know.

_____

_____

_____

_____

❹ IMAGINE What do you think it would be like to see a ghost on stage at the beginning of a play? What kind of **atmosphere** would the ghost's presence create?

_____

_____

_____

_____

❺ In general, why do you think writers use foreshadowing? You may use the excerpts from *A Tale of Two Cities* and *Hamlet* as examples. Write as much or as little as you need to. You do not have to use this entire page, and you can use additional sheets if necessary.

_____

_____

_____

_____

_____

_____

_____

_____

_____

_____

_____

_____

_____

_____

_____

_____

_____

_____

_____

_____

12. IMAGERY

When a vivid mental image is developed with words

The Persian poet Rumi once wrote, "Close both eyes/to see with the other eye." We see with our "other eye" when we encounter imagery. Imagery usually refers to the use of words to create a mental image, but it can also refer to words that appeal to the other senses, of smell, touch, taste, and hearing. Although we don't find real sights, sounds, tastes, or smells in books, imagery makes us feel as if we do.

Ezra Pound uses imagery to capture the experience of emerging from a crowded train in his poem "In a Station of the Metro."

> *"The apparition of these faces in the crowd;*
> *Petals on a wet, black bough."*

In this example, Pound recounts a true story for his readers, but he doesn't give a literal account of what he *saw*. Instead, he constructs images that convey how he felt as he left the train and stepped onto the platform. When we envision "petals on a wet, black bough" and transplant that image onto an image of a crowd, we can feel something similar to what Pound felt that day.

Walt Whitman also uses imagery in the following poem:

> *"When I heard the learn'd astronomer,*
> *When the proofs, the figures, were ranged in columns before me,*
> *When I was shown the charts and diagrams, to add, divide, and measure them…"*

With his words, Whitman conjures up an image of an astronomer, surrounded by a sea of diagrams and mathematical equations. The astronomer isn't actually looking up at the sky. Whitman soon grows tired of the scientist.

> *"How soon unaccountable I became tired and sick,*
> *Till rising and gliding out I wander'd off by myself,*
> *In the mystical moist night-air, and from time to time,*
> *Look'd up in perfect silence at the stars."*

> —"When I Heard the Learn'd Astronomer," by Walt Whitman

The poet prefers the image of the sky itself and the feelings it gives him to the "charts and diagrams" of the astronomer. The "charts and diagrams" can't tell us much about "mystical moist night-air."

As with Whitman and Pound, writers choose to use imagery to show how they feel about a subject. When they do this, they appeal to the "other eye" of their readers.

Understanding IMAGERY

❶ ANALYZE Why do you think Pound uses the word "apparition" in the poem "In a Station of the Metro"?

_____

_____

_____

_____

❷ DESCRIBE How would describe the **atmosphere,** or overall feeling, of "In a Station of the Metro"?

_____

_____

_____

_____

❸ MAKE A LIST Which senses does Whitman appeal to in "When I Heard the Learn'd Astronomer"?

_____

_____

_____

❹ DESCRIBE Describe the **atmosphere** of "When I Heard the Learn'd Astronomer." How do the images in the poem contribute to this atmosphere?

_____

_____

_____

_____

_____

❺ In her poem "Like the Very Gods," the Greek poet Sappho describes being dumbstruck in the presence of the one she loves.

*"Nothing shows in front of my eyes, my ears are
muted in thunder."*

Do you think this is an example of imagery, even though the narrator of the poem cannot see or hear? Why or why not? Write as much or as little as you need to. You do not have to use this entire page, and you can use additional sheets if necessary.

_____

_____

_____

_____

_____

_____

_____

_____

_____

_____

_____

_____

_____

_____

_____

_____

_____

_____

13. INVERSION

*Writing a sentence out of its normal order, particularly when
the subject and predicate, or verb clause, are switched*

Sometimes a sentence can be turned on its head and still be readable. A sentence is inverted when the subject and the predicate—the verb and the whole phrase associated with the verb—are thrown into a surprisingly orderly state of disorder.

The following translation of "Psalm 23" uses inversion several times, and though we are not as accustomed to the way it sounds, it is still understandable and even beautiful.

> *"The Lord to me a shepherd is,*
> *want therefore shall not I:*
> *He in the folds of tender grass,*
> *Doth cause me down to lie."*

> —from "Psalm 23," from the Bay Psalm Book

The inversion in this psalm has several purposes. For one, it slows us down; it takes a bit more time to read through its unorthodox *diction,* or word choice. The reader becomes more meditative, pausing on each word and on each thought. Inversion also allows for the second and fourth lines to **rhyme,** and **rhyme** is pleasant to the ear.

A.E. Housman also uses inversion in the poem "Eight O'Clock."

> *"He stood, and heard the steeple*
> *Sprinkle the quarters on the morning town.*
> *One, two, three, four, to market-place and people*
> *It tossed them down."*

This verse ends with inversion. Instead of writing, "it tossed them down to market-place and people," Housman writes, "to market-place and people/It tossed them down." The next verse also ends with an inverted sentence.

> *"Strapped, noosed, nighing his hour,*
> *He stood and counted them and cursed his luck;*
> *And then the clock collected in the tower*
> *Its strength, and struck."*

The inversion in this poem conveniently fits Housman's words into an abab cdcd **rhyme** scheme. But it is also appropriate to the description of a clock. As in "Psalm 23", this inversion slows us down. Housman uses this to describe how a clock moves slowly and painstakingly from minute to minute. Inversion is just one of the ways writers can use the sound and the visual effect of words to convey their message.

❶ *DEMONSTRATE* Rewrite the excerpt from Psalm 23 without using inversion.

_____

_____

_____

_____

❷ *COMPARE/CONTRAST* Read your version of Psalm 23 and the version on the previous page aloud. Are the overall effects of each version different?

_____

_____

_____

_____

❸ *EXPLAIN* What do you think happens when the clock collects its strength and strikes?

_____

_____

_____

_____

❹ *DISCUSS* Housman writes, "And then the clock collected in the tower/Its strength, and struck." Why did Housman choose to use inversion in this line, aside from considerations of **rhyme?**

_____

_____

_____

_____

_____

❺ Choose a few lines from a poem you have read recently, or find one online or in a book. Use inversion to rewrite those lines; see if you can invert the words in more than one way. Do not feel obligated to fill the entire page, or be limited by it. Use additional paper if you need to. Write as much or as little as you need to.

14. IRONY

*A contrast or incongruity between what is stated and what it meant,
or between what is expected and what actually happens*

With irony, one should expect the unexpected. Writers play off of the difference between what you think will happen and what actually happens or the difference between what someone says and what they mean. These differences can either turn into something funny or into something serious.

Verbal irony is used when a character or narrator means something other than he or she says. The following poem is an example of sarcasm, a type of verbal irony.

> *"The toughness indoor people have:*
> *the will*
> *to brave confusion in*
> *mohair sofas, crocheted doilies—challenging*
> *in every tidy corner some*
> *bit of the outdoor drift and sag."*
>
> —from "Birthday Card to My Mother," by Philip Appleman

Appleman is not actually saying that "indoor people" are brave. Instead, he shows it would be ridiculous to think of people who refuse to go outside as warriors. The incongruity, or the dissimilarity between what he says and what he means makes the poem funny.

Situational irony refers to surprising or unexpected occurrences. The situational irony begins almost as soon as the following poem begins.

> *"There was an old man from Calcutta,*
> *Who coated his tonsils with butta,*
> *Thus converting his snore*
> *From a thunderous roar*
> *To a soft, oleaginous mutta."*
>
> —"Arthur," by Ogden Nash

We read the first line, accepting that there's an old man from Calcutta. What happens in the second line, though, is quite unexpected. The idea of a man confronting his snoring problem with "butta" is not one we would think of normally. The ironic humor of this poem feels random and goofy, like an episode of "Monty Python."

Although irony is often humorous, it can also address dark **themes.** Verbal irony, and especially sarcasm, can be cruel, and the unexpected occurrences caused by situational irony can be tragic. It all depends on how an author exploits the difference between the expected and the unexpected, or between what is said and what is meant.

Understanding IRONY

❶ *IN YOUR OWN WORDS* Summarize the poem, "Birthday Card to My Mother."

_____

_____

_____

❷ *ANALYZE* Appleman says that "indoor people" are courageous enough to "brave confusion in/mohair sofas." What do you think he means by this? What confusion are they battling?

_____

_____

_____

_____

❸ *ELEMENTAL CONNECTION* Is it important that the poem "Arthur" follows a **rhyme** scheme?

_____

_____

_____

_____

❹ *EXPLAIN* Why might the narrator of "Arthur" have an accent?

_____

_____

_____

_____

_____

❺ Write several statements that are verbally ironic. Write as much or as little as you need to. You do not have to use this entire page, and you can use additional sheets if necessary.

_____

_____

_____

_____

_____

_____

_____

_____

_____

_____

_____

_____

_____

_____

_____

_____

_____

_____

_____

_____

_____

_____

15. METAPHOR

A direct comparison of two dissimilar things

According to novelist John Gardner, "every metaphor…ties the imagined to the fully experienced." Metaphors, like **similes** and **analogies,** compare things that technically shouldn't be compared. They squish mismatched things together.

Unlike **similes,** metaphors don't use words of comparison such as *like* or *as.* Instead, one thing actually starts to become another thing in our imagination.

The narrator of the poem "Metaphors" undergoes many metaphorical changes.

> *"I'm a riddle in nine syllables,*
> *An elephant, a ponderous house,*
> *A melon strolling on two tendrils.*
> *O red fruit, ivory, fine timbers!*
> *This loaf's big with its yeasty rising.*
> *Money's new-minted in this fat purse.*
> *I'm a means, a stage, a cow in calf.*
> *I've eaten a bag of green apples,*
> *Boarded the train there's no getting off."*

—from "Metaphors," by Sylvia Plath

It's surprising that a person could imagine themselves being like so many different things, from a riddle to a cow, but that shows the power and dexterity of the metaphor. All of these diverse metaphors lead to the last line, "I've…boarded the train there's no getting off." Now we know she feels weighed down with some kind of inevitability, an inability to change her fate.

William Blake's poem "To See a World in a Grain of Sand" also uses metaphors.

> *"To see a world in a grain of sand*
> *And a heaven in a wild flower,*
> *Hold infinity in the palm of your hand*
> *And eternity in an hour."*

It's not possible, of course, to actually see a whole world in a grain of sand, or heaven in a flower. But Blake asserts that even the smallest parts of nature can reveal something about the eternal.

We learn about ourselves and how we relate to our surroundings when we use metaphors. They help us notice connections between disparate things and allow us to be creative with the "fully experienced." With a metaphor in mind, it's not so crazy to think that you could hold infinity in your hand.

Understanding METAPHOR

❶ ANALYZE Consider the metaphors used in Sylvia Plath's poem. How do you think the narrator feels in this poem?

_____

_____

_____

❷ DESCRIBE What is "a riddle in nine syllables" like?

_____

_____

_____

_____

❸ EXPLAIN What do you think it means to "see a world in a grain of sand/And a heaven in a wild flower"?

_____

_____

_____

_____

❹ REFLECT Have you ever experienced something like what the narrator of "To See a World in a Grain of Sand" feels in this poem? Describe the feeling.

_____

_____

_____

_____

Writing About METAPHOR

❺ The writer Jorge Luis Borges once wrote, "We came upon the metaphor, the invocation by which we disordered the rigid universe." Explain what Borges might mean. Do you think that metaphors "disorder" the world around us, or do they make things seem clearer and more orderly? Could they do both of these things? Write as much or as little as you need to. You do not have to use this entire page, and you can use additional sheets if necessary.

16. METER

The patterned repeating of stressed and unstressed syllables

There's no need to feel stressed out about meter. Usually, the metrical forms used in poetry imitate our speech and our songs. The metrical form used most commonly in English is *iambic pentameter*. A foot is the most basic unit of meter. It consists of one or two unstressed syllables and one stressed syllable. When there are five feet in a line of verse, or ten syllables usually, the meter of that line is called "pentameter."

An *iamb* is a type of foot that consists of an unstressed syllable followed by a stressed syllable. You will encounter iambic pentameter again and again. Shakespeare wrote all of his **sonnets** and most of his plays in iambic pentameter, and it is still popular. Iambic pentameter may be a form, or a set of rules, that's imposed on a poem; for all that, though, iambic pentameter sounds natural. It's not an arbitrary, or random, rule.

The following poem adheres very closely, though not entirely, to iambic pentameter. (Because the first line has 12 syllables.)

> *"Now faces the glimmering landscape on the sight,*
> *And all the air a solemn stillness holds,*
> *Save where the beetle wheels his droning flight,*
> *And drowsy tinklings lull the distant folds…"*

> —from "Elegy Written in a Country Churchyard," by Thomas Gray

Like "Elegy," Robert Frost's poem "Mending Wall" is written in iambic pentameter. The narrator of this poem is repairing a wall with his neighbor.

> *"He moves in darkness as it seems to me—*
> *Not of woods only and the shade of trees.*
> *He will not go behind his father's saying,*
> *And he likes having thought of it so well*
> *He says again, 'Good fences make good neighbors.'"*

Unlike Gray's poem, "Mending Wall" does not follow a **rhyme** scheme. It's written in *blank verse,* or verse that is in iambic pentameter but that does not **rhyme.**

Listening for meter in a poem is like listening for the key and time signature in music. The more and more you try to consciously analyze music, instead of just listening it, the more familiar you will become with the individual sounds. Try doing the same with meter in poems, and you will be able to hear how words have a **rhythm** that is naturally pleasing to the ear.

Understanding METER

❶ SCAN IT *Scansion* is a metrical analysis of a poem that identifies the stressed syllables (/) and unstressed syllables (˘). Complete a scansion of the excerpts from Thomas Gray's "Elegy."

Here is a scansion of the first line of "Elegy."

˘ / ˘ / ˘ / ˘ / ˘ /

_____

_____

_____

❷ ELEMENTAL CONNECTION What atmosphere, or overall feeling, is evoked by the excerpt from "Elegy"?

_____

_____

_____

_____

❸ SCAN IT Scan the first two lines from Robert Frost's "Mending Wall."

_____

_____

❹ IDENTIFY An iamb is a foot consisting of an unstressed syllable followed by a stressed one, while a *trochee* consists of a stressed syllable followed by an unstressed syllable. Can you think of two words that are iambic, and two words that are trochaic?

_____

_____

_____

5 The excerpt from "Elegy" describes a scene in nature. Write a four-line verse about a place in nature using iambic pentameter and an abab **rhyme** scheme.

_____

_____

_____

_____

_____

_____

_____

_____

_____

_____

_____

_____

_____

_____

_____

_____

_____

_____

_____

_____

_____

17. ONOMATOPOEIA

Using words to imitate sounds associated
with a thing or an action

You may think that you only read with your eyes, but you also read with your ears. Good writers keep the sounds of words in mind as they write, and some use onomatopoeias, which sound like the things they name or represent. Some examples of onomatopoeias are *splash*, *plop*, and *ring*.

Edgar Allen Poe uses ordinary words that evoke the **rhythm** and feeling of sleigh bells in his poem "The Bells."

> *"What a world of merriment their melody foretells!*
> *How they tinkle, tinkle, tinkle,*
> *In the icy air of night!"*

By repeating the word *tinkle,* he makes readers hear the sleigh bells in their minds. Poe describes the bells further, as they are:

> *"Keeping time, time, time,*
> *In a sort of Runic rhyme,*
> *To the tintinnabulation that so musically wells*
> *From the bells, bells, bells, bells,*
> *Bells, bells, bells…"*

Poe actually creates a new word, *tintinnabulation,* which is specifically meant to sound like the merry music of sleigh bells. Readers can easily imagine themselves riding in a sleigh, listening to its festive jingle.

John Updike uses onomatopoeias in his story "A&P" just as effectively as Poe does, if not as merrily. The narrator of the story, a grocery clerk named Sammy, mentally sings along to the sounds of a cash register.

> *"I go through the punches, 4, 9, GROC, TOT—it's more complicated than you think, and*
> *after you do it often enough, it begins to make a little song, that you hear words to, in my*
> *case, 'Hello (bing) there, you (gung) hap-py pee-pul (splat)!'—the splat being the drawer*
> *flying out."*

Because of Updike's clever use of onomatopoeias, we feel like we're at that cash register with Sammy. While we read, we go through the motions of being a grocery clerk with him. It is in the same way, Poe helps us to imagine ourselves riding in a sleigh on a winter night.

❶ DESCRIBE   How would you describe the atmosphere, or mood, of "The Bells"?

_____

_____

_____

❷ YOU DECIDE   Read "The Bells" aloud. Do you think that the onomatopoeias in this poem successfully capture the "world of merriment" created by the sleigh bells? Justify your answer.

_____

_____

_____

_____

❸ ANALYZE   Refer to the excerpt from "A&P" on the previous page. How do you think Sammy feels about his job?

_____

_____

_____

_____

❹ RESEARCH   The previous page lists a few onomatopoeias that are commonly used. Can you think of any more examples? Or can you create a few onomatopoeias of your own?

_____

_____

_____

_____

_____

❺ In general, why do you think a writer would use onomatopoeias? What effect do they have on readers? Write as much or as little as you need to. You do not have to use this entire page, and you can use additional sheets if necessary.

18. PERSONIFICATION

*When an animal, object, or an abstract concept
is given human qualities*

Who hasn't cursed at a computer as if it had a conscience, or spoken to a dog as if he understood English? When we do this, we personify the objects, animals, and ideas that surround us. This tendency of ours shows up in all kinds of literature as well as in all walks of life.

Carl Sandburg personifies the future, an abstract concept, in the poem "Four Preludes on Playthings of the Wind."

> *"The woman named Tomorrow*
> *sits with a hairpin in her teeth*
> *and takes her time*
> *and does her hair the way she wants it*
> *and fastens at last the last braid and coil*
> *and puts the hairpin where it belongs*
> *and turns and drawls: Well, what of it?*
> *My grandmother, Yesterday, is gone.*
> *What of it? Let the dead be dead."*

Sandburg turns Tomorrow into a human character, with the mannerisms and movements of a matter-of-fact woman. By using personification here, Sandburg persuades his reader to think of the future in a certain way. It is no longer just an idea that is hard to comprehend and therefore frightening, but a person who might even get on our nerves.

Some authors also use personification to forge a link between people and nature. William Blake speaks to a fly, almost as if to a child, saying:

> *"Little fly,*
> *Thy summer's play*
> *My thoughtless hand*
> *Has brushed away.*
>
> *Am not I*
> *A fly like thee?*
> *Or art not thou*
> *A man like me?"*

> —from "The Fly," by William Blake

According to Blake, flies and people might not be too different. Most people wonder, from time to time, if animals think and feel like we do. We end up thinking about inanimate objects and ideas in the same way. As we try to unlock the world around us, we use personification to try to grapple with nature and intangible ideas.

Understanding PERSONIFICATION

❶ *ELEMENTAL CONNECTION* What kind of **tone,** or attitude, does Sandburg take towards Tomorrow as a character? How does he feel about the future in general?

_____

_____

_____

_____

❷ *ANALYZE* In William Blake's "The Fly," what kind of character does the fly remind you of, and why?

_____

_____

_____

_____

❸ *INFER* What thoughts might have prompted Blake to ask the question, "Am not I/A fly like thee?/Or art not thou/A man like me?"

_____

_____

_____

_____

❹ *RESEARCH* Identify an example of personification in poetry or prose.

_____

_____

_____

_____

5 A few reasons for using personification were given on a previous page. Can you think of any more? If possible, give examples to support your answers. The examples can either be original or from another piece of writing. Write as much or as little as you need to. You do not have to use this entire page, and you can use additional sheets if necessary.

_____

_____

_____

_____

_____

_____

_____

_____

_____

_____

_____

_____

_____

_____

_____

_____

_____

_____

_____

_____

_____

_____

_____

19. PLOT

*The sequence of events or actions that make up
a short story, novel, narrative poem, or play*

The plot of a story, novel, play, or poem consists of many different elements, including *exposition, conflict, rising action, climax, falling action,* and *resolution.* Understanding the framework in which all of these separate elements fit together is crucial when trying to understand literature.

It may help to visualize the plot of a story as a rising and descending staircase; the story builds in tension until it reaches the top of the staircase, or the *climax,* and finally resolves itself at the end, at the bottom of the descending staircase.

In the *exposition* stage of a story, an author will provide all of the information necessary for the reader to understand what happens next. As a story opens, we usually encounter a description of the main character or the setting. We may also learn about any past events that will affect the course of the story later on. If we continue with our staircase analogy, this is the part of the story where we learn what the stairs look like.

Just as no life is free of problems, no story is free of *conflict.* A conflict, or a struggle of some kind, can be internal or external. An internal conflict comes about when a character feels pulled in several directions and cannot decide how to act. An external conflict is created when a character struggles with forces outside of him or herself. It may be between two people, or between one person and a whole society, or one person against nature. A conflict introduces tension to a story, which arises from the struggle of opposing forces. The tension builds as the story goes on, and eventually the story reaches a *climax,* where tension and excitement are at their highest.

Sometimes a climax and the conflict which causes it will appear from out of the blue. At other times, many small events caused by conflicting elements gradually lead to the climax. These events are part of the *rising action.*

After the climax, the story goes through a phase of *falling action,* where the tension and intensity of the climax begins to decrease.

The next stage of a story is known as the dénouement or *resolution.* In French, *dénouement* refers to the untying of a knot. At this stage, the story begins to unwind itself and comes to a conclusion.

❶ *INDENTIFY* Identify the conflict in a story of your choosing. Name the story and identify the conflict.

_____

_____

_____

_____

❷ *SUMMARIZE* Summarize the rising action in the story.

_____

_____

_____

_____

❸ *DESCRIBE* What happens at the story's climax?

_____

_____

_____

_____

❹ *SUMMARIZE* Summarize the falling action and resolution of the story.

_____

_____

_____

_____

_____

5 Do you think there could be a good story that doesn't contain any conflict? Why or why not? Write as much or as little as you need to. You do not have to use this entire page, and you can use additional sheets if necessary.

_____

_____

_____

_____

_____

_____

_____

_____

_____

_____

_____

_____

_____

_____

_____

_____

_____

_____

_____

_____

_____

_____

_____

20. POINT OF VIEW

Point of view, speaker, or persona refers to the imagined person who tells a story or poem

A story can be told from several perspectives. Each of these perspectives can greatly impact a story. A *first-person point of view* actively participates in the poem and uses first-person pronouns like "I" and "me."

> "1, 2, 3, 4,
> *My shoes don't fit in these four tracks.*
> *If my shoes don't fit in these four tracks,*
> *whose tracks are they?*
> *A shark's?*
> *A new-born elephant's? A duck's?*
> *A flea's? A quail's?"*
>
> —from "Buster Keaton Looks in the Woods for His Love Who Is a Real Cow," by Rafael Alberti

A *third-person, omniscient point of view* does not actively participate in the poem, presents the poem from an all-knowing perspective, and uses third-person pronouns like "she" and "him."

> "*There was an Old Man who supposed,*
> *That the street door was partially closed;*
> *But some very large rats,*
> *ate his coats and his hats,*
> *While that futile old gentleman dozed.*"
>
> —"There Was an Old Man Who Supposed," by Edward Lear

A *third-person, limited point of view* does not actively participate in the poem, presents the poem from one or a few characters' perspectives, and uses third-person pronouns like "she" and "him," as in this anonymous poem, "The Village Burglar."

> "*The burglar is a hairy man*
> *With whickers round his eyes.*
>
> *He goes to church on Sundays;*
> *He hears the Parson shout;*
> *He puts a penny in the plate*
> *And takes a shilling out.*"

As you can see, it makes a huge difference who the narrator is because each kind of narrator has different kinds of insight. As you read a story or a poem, you should always remember who is telling it.

❶ IDENTIFY Given the title of the poem, "Buster Keaton Looks in the Woods for His Love Who Is a Real Cow," who is narrating the poem?

_____

❷ RESEARCH Use the internet or your school's library to research the life of Buster Keaton. Based on what you find, what is Rafael Alberti's **tone,** or attitude, towards the narrator of this poem?

_____

_____

_____

_____

❸ ANALYZE The poem "There Was an Old Man Who Supposed" is written from an omniscient or all-knowing perspective. How can you tell this from the poem?

_____

_____

_____

_____

❹ COMPARE/CONTRAST "There Was an Old Man Who Supposed" and "The Village Burglar" are both written from the third person point of view, but one is omniscient while the other is not. How does this cause the two poems to differ?

_____

_____

_____

_____

_____

5 Write about something funny that happened to you from the three different perspectives discussed on the previous page. Write a paragraph for each perspective. Write as much or as little as you need to. You do not have to use this entire page, and you can use additional sheets if necessary.

_____

_____

_____

_____

_____

_____

_____

_____

_____

_____

_____

_____

_____

_____

_____

_____

_____

_____

_____

_____

_____

_____

_____

21. REFRAIN

*A refrain or chorus is a phrase or verse that appears
at regular intervals throughout a poem*

Ezra Pound once said that "poetry begins to atrophy," or decay, "when it gets too far from music." Many poets seem to agree with Pound, and they write poems that could almost be set to music. One of the ways poems are made more songlike is through the use of a refrain, a phrase that is repeated throughout the poem.

Perhaps one of the most famous refrains in poetry is from Edgar Allen Poe's poem "The Raven."

> *"'Be that word our sign of parting, bird or fiend!' I shrieked upstarting—*
> *'Get thee back into the tempest and the Night's Plutonian shore!*
> *Leave no black plume as a token of that lie thy soul hath spoken!*
> *Leave my loneliness unbroken! - quit the bust above my door!*
> *Take thy beak from out my heart, and take thy form from off my door!'*
> *Quoth the raven, 'Nevermore.'"*

A raven taunts a young man with the word "Nevermore," at the end of each verse. The young man, already in mourning for his beloved Lenore, becomes increasingly disturbed each time the Raven speaks. Readers, too, can sense the young man growing more and more desperate at the sound of each "Nevermore."

The refrain in "The Raven" derives much of its power from repetition. At the end of every verse, we are reminded of the young man's hopelessness.

The following poem by Pablo Neruda also includes a refrain, but a much less feverish one.

> *"Tonight I can write the saddest lines.*
>
> *Write for example, 'The night is shattered*
> *and the blue stars shiver in the distance.'*
>
> *The night wind revolves in the sky and sings.*
>
> *Tonight I can write the saddest lines.*
> *I loved her, and sometimes she loved me too."*
>
> — from "Tonight I Can Write the Saddest Lines," by Pablo Neruda

In this poem, the refrain serves as a resting place for the reader. The narrator shares a few broken moments of his experience with us, and we return, revolving like the night wind, to the refrain. Refrains in many poems and songs are like Neruda's "tonight I can write the saddest lines;" after each verse, we return to the refrain, having learned something new from the verse.

❶ *ANALYZE* The narrator of "The Raven" is mourning the loss of a woman he loves, Lenore. Is it significant that her name rhymes with the word "Nevermore"?

_____

_____

_____

❷ *EXPLAIN* Why does the narrator of "The Raven" tell the raven to "leave [his] loneliness unbroken"?

_____

_____

_____

_____

❸ *DISCUSS* The narrator of Neruda's poem offers these lines as an example of the "saddest lines."

"…The night is shattered
And the blue stars shiver in the distance."

How would you interpret these lines, and why are they sad?

_____

_____

_____

❹ *ELEMENTAL CONNECTION* How would you describe the **atmosphere,** or overall feeling, of "Tonight I Can Write the Saddest Lines"?

_____

_____

_____

_____

❺ Find a poem either in your school's library or online that has a refrain. Copy it here, and then analyze how the repitition of the refrain affects the overall feeling of the poem. Write as much or as little as you need to. You do not have to use this entire page, and you can use additional sheets if necessary.

22. RHYME

*The repetition of sounds in two or more words
that appear close to each other*

According to Samuel Butler, rhyme is "the rudder" of verses, "with which like ships they steer their course." When a poet faces the challenge of the blank page, a rhyme scheme is a helpful framework. With a rhyme scheme in place, the poem seems to write itself. This is one of the many reasons that poets, songwriters, and children turn to rhyme.

- There are several different ways to use rhyme. An *exact rhyme* repeats the sounds exactly.

    "By lions' jaws great benefits and blessings were begotten
    And so our debt to Lionhood must never be forgotten."

    —from "Sunt Leones," by Stevie Smith

- In an *approximate rhyme* or *slant rhyme*, the repeated sounds are similar but not the same.

    "Not magnitude, not lavishness,
    But form—the site;
    Not innovating wilfulness,
    But reverence for the archetype."

    —from "Greek Architecture," by Herman Melville

- A rhyme that occurs at the ends of lines is called an *end rhyme*, as in "A Bookmark," by Tom Disch.

    "Four years ago I started reading Proust.
    Although I'm past the halfway point, I still
    Have seven hundred pages of reduced
    Type left before I reach the end. I will
    Slog through…"

- A rhyme that occurs within a line is called an *internal rhyme*, as in the poem "The Walloping Window-Blind," by Charles Edward Carryl.

    "A capitol ship for an ocean trip
    Was The Walloping Window-Blind—
    No gale that blew dismayed her crew
    Or troubled the captain's mind."

The internal rhyme scheme of this poem is appropriately light and playful. Like Carryl, poets try to match the sound of the rhyme of the poem they're writing with its meaning.

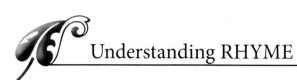

Understanding RHYME

❶ ANALYZE Do end rhyme and internal rhyme have different effects? Use examples from the previous page.

_____

_____

_____

❷ COMPARE/CONTRAST How would you compare the slant rhyme used in Melville's poem to the exact rhyme of Smith's "Sunt Leones"? Could the sounds they create affect readers differently?

_____

_____

_____

_____

❸ EXPLAIN In "A Bookmark," the last three lines end in accordance with the a b a b rhyme scheme, but Disch doesn't finish his thoughts in each of these lines. Why do you think Disch does this?

_____

_____

_____

_____

❹ HEARING IT ALOUD Read "The Walloping Window-Blind" aloud. How would you describe how the poem sounds?

_____

_____

_____

_____

Writing Using RHYME

5 Write a short poem using rhyme at least twice. Write as much or as little as you need to. You do not have to use this entire page, and you can use additional sheets if necessary.

23. RHYTHM

*The natural, non-repeating pattern of stressed
and unstressed syllables in a poem*

If you've ever read something that set your toes to tapping, you were probably noticing the natural rhythm of the words. For most words, we emphasize some of the syllables, causing them to seem a bit longer, or a little bit louder, than unstressed syllables. Stressed syllables and unstressed syllables alternate, together forming a kind of dance, a sound pattern, which is similar to the pattern we hear in music.

When rhythm and **rhyme** come together in a poem, the effect is even more musical. Countee Cullen's poem "Heritage" uses a strong natural rhythm and rhyming **couplets;** the overall effect makes readers want to read the poem aloud.

> *"What is Africa to me:*
> *Copper sun or scarlet sea,*
> *Jungle star or jungle track,*
> *Strong bronzed men, or regal black*
> *Women from whose loins I sprang*
> *When the birds of Eden sang?...*
> *Spicy grove, cinnamon tree,*
> *What is Africa to me?"*

The **imagery** of this poem could speak for itself, but the rhythm of the words makes the poem's voice even stronger.

The rhythm of Gwendlyn Brooks' poem "We Real Cool" imitates the speech of adolescent boys who feel like they are on top of the world.

> *"We real cool. We*
> *Left school. We*
>
> *Lurk late. We*
> *Strike straight. We*
>
> *Sing sin. We*
> *Thin gin. We*
>
> *Jazz June. We*
> *Die soon."*

The visual format of Brooks' poem causes readers to pause after each, "We," creating a rhythm which echoes jazz music but also sounds like the voices of young boys, trying to sound cool. Both Brooks and Cullen use rhythm to create compelling poetry.

❶ ANALYZE Cullen's poem "Heritage" asks a question—"What is Africa to Me?"—but doesn't really answer it. Do you feel like the rhythm of the poem suits this uncertainty?

_____

_____

_____

❷ ELEMENTAL CONNECTION Would the overall effect of "Heritage" have been different if it had the same rhythm, but was not written with rhyming **couplets?**

_____

_____

_____

_____

❸ HEARING IT ALOUD Read the poem, "We Real Cool," aloud to yourself. Then listen to a recording of Brooks reading the poem (try http://www.poets.org/viewmedia.php/prmMID/15433). Why do you think Brooks ended so many lines without finishing her thought, but by simply saying "We" at the end of each line? How does this affect the rhythm?

_____

_____

_____

_____

❹ INTERPRET The poem "We Real Cool" is about boys in a pool hall. What is Brooks' **tone,** or attitude, towards the boys?

_____

_____

_____

❺ Do you know any song that has lyrics with a good rhythm? Obtain a copy of the lyrics and write about the rhythm of the lyrics. Write as much or as little as you need to. You do not have to use this entire page, and you can use additional sheets if necessary.

_____

_____

_____

_____

_____

_____

_____

_____

_____

_____

_____

_____

_____

_____

_____

_____

_____

_____

_____

_____

_____

_____

24. SIMILE

A direct comparison of two things using either the word "like" or "as"

Like **metaphors** and **analogies,** similes compare two different things which, at first glance, seem to have little in common. Similes can be distinguished from metaphors and analogies, though, because they contain the words "like" or "as."

Langston Hughes constructs his poem "Harlem" on a foundation laid by similes.

> *"What happens to a dream deferred?*
>
> *Does it dry up*
> *like a raisin in the sun?*
> *Or fester like a sore—*
> *And then run?*
> *Does it stink like rotten meat?*
> *Or crust and sugar over—*
> *like a syrupy sweet?...*
>
> *Or does it explode?"*

Hughes never really answers the question. The reader can guess what happens to a dream that's "deferred," or delayed, but never with too much certainty. The ambiguity here makes an important point—that a dream never acted upon can be likened to many things. Perhaps it can pass quickly from drying up "like a raisin in the sun" to sugaring over "like a syrupy sweet," until it finally explodes. All of these similes, added together, paint a picture of frustration, frustration that changes its face too often to be fully nailed down and analyzed.

Similes can also feel more ethereal than they do in Hughes' poem.

> *"Life, like a dome of many-colored glass,*
> *Stains the white radiance of Eternity."*
>
> — from "Adonais," by Percy Bysshe Shelley

Life stains the light of Eternity, but in a special way. It doesn't stain the eternal light in the way things are usually stained. Our mortal life is like a stained-glass window that filters the eternal light, refracting it and spreading it to the many parts of our existence.

Hughes and Shelley provide us with good examples of similes, but their examples represent only a few of the many ways similes that can be used.

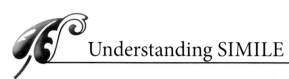

❶ *MAKE A LIST* List all of the similes in "Harlem." Choose one of them. Why do you think Hughes uses this image to describe a "dream deferred"?

_____

_____

_____

_____

_____

❷ *IN YOUR OWN WORDS* Explain what the poem "Harlem" means in your own words.

_____

_____

_____

_____

_____

❸ *ANALYZE* Why do you think life "stains the white radiance of Eternity" like "a dome of many-colored glass" in Shelley's "Adonais"?

_____

_____

_____

_____

_____

❹ *RESEARCH* Find three different similes in other books, poems, or songs.

_____

_____

_____

5 What do you think makes a good simile? What makes it convincing and compelling? Use the provided examples or, your list from Question 4. Write as much or as little as you need to. You do not have to use this entire page, and you can use additional sheets if necessary.

_____

_____

_____

_____

_____

_____

_____

_____

_____

_____

_____

_____

_____

_____

_____

_____

_____

_____

_____

_____

_____

_____

_____

25. SONNET

A poem of 14 lines, usually written in iambic pentameter

Sonnets allow poets to sing. From the Italian word for "little song" *(sonneto),* sonnets have been written through the ages. From Shakespeare, who wrote 154 sonnets, to modern poets, this poetic, songlike form has never lost popularity.

The *Shakespearean sonnet,* or the *English sonnet,* consists of three *quatrains* and one **couplet.** The **rhyme** scheme is abab cdcd efef gg, as in this "Sonnet 12" by William Shakespeare.

> *"When I do count the clock that tell the time,*
> *And see the brave day sunk in hideous night;*
> *When I behold the violet past prime,*
> *And sable curls, all silvered o'er with white;*
> *When lofty trees I see barren of leaves,*
> *Which erst from heat did canopy the herd,*
> *And summer's green all girded up in sheaves,*
> *Borne on the bier with white and bristly beard,*
> *Then of thy beauty do I question make,*
> *That thou among the wastes of time must go,*
> *Since sweets and beauties do themselves forsake*
> *And die as fast as they see others grow;*
> *And nothing 'gainst time's scythe can make defense*
> *Save breed, to brave him when he takes thee hence."*

In "Sonnet 12," Shakespeare addresses a question he addresses in many of his sonnets: how does one make love last? Although this one **theme** shows up in many of Shakespeare's sonnet, it's just one of the possible topics than can inspire a sonnet.

Shakespeare and other Enlish sonneteers were inspired by *Petrarchan,* or *Italian sonnets*. It consists of an *octave* (or two quatrains) and a *sestet,* or six lines. The rhyme scheme is abba abba cde cde. Another British poet, John Milton, wrote the Petrarchan sonnet "On His Blindness." Here is the ending sestet from that sonnet, which is about Milton's struggle with blindness.

> *"...But Patience to prevent*
> *That murmur, soon replies, 'God doth not need*
> *Either man's work or his own gifts; who best*
> *Bear his mild yoke, they serve him best. His state*
> *Is Kingly. Thousands at his bidding speed*
> *And post o'er land and ocean without rest;*
> *They also serve who only stand and wait."*

Milton and Shakespeare show that sonnets can address a wide range of topics, from the insecurities of love to blindness and religion.

Understanding SONNETS

❶ IN YOUR OWN WORDS Summarize Shakespeare's "Sonnet 12."

_____

_____

_____

_____

_____

_____

❷ YOU DECIDE Is "Sonnet 12" songlike? Why or why not?

_____

_____

_____

❸ ANALYZE The first three quatrains of "Sonnet 12" list all of the bad effects of time passing. Then, in the last ending **couplet,** Shakespeare says there's nothing that can stand up to time "save breed," or procreation. Do you think that having children could make up for the losses listed in the first 12 lines of the poem?

_____

_____

_____

_____

❹ EXPLAIN What do you think Milton means when he says, "They also serve who only stand and wait"?

_____

_____

_____

_____

_____

Writing a SONNET

5 Write a Shakespearean or Petrarchan sonnet on any topic, following the proper **rhyme** scheme. If you'd like, write your own sonnet about the passage of time.

_____

_____

_____

_____

_____

_____

_____

_____

_____

_____

_____

_____

_____

_____

_____

_____

_____

_____

_____

_____

_____

_____

_____

_____

_____

26. STYLE

*The unique qualities that make a single writer,
a literary group, or period distinct*

Good writers have style. From their *diction,* or choice of words, to their sentence construction and use of **figurative language,** these writers are not afraid to show their individuality.

Emily Dickinson's poem "986" shows that she was such a writer.

> "A narrow Fellow in the Grass
> Occassionally rides—
> You may have met him—did you not
> His notice sudden is—"

Her style includes the use of dashes (—) to separate thoughts which in this poem are very fragmented. In the third line, there is a striking absence of a question mark after the question, "did you not," and she uses **inversion,** or an inverted word order, in the phrase, "His notice sudden is."

E.E. Cummings was also famous for his distinctive style. He played around with punctuation and didn't capitalize words when he technically should have. The following poem, "l(a," displays many of Cummings' trademarks, but its style is also specifically tailored for its subject, loneliness.

> "l(a
>
> le
> af
> fa
>
> ll
>
> s)
> one
> l
>
> iness"

Instead of writing "l(a leaf falls)oneliness," Cummings isolates the letters from each other. The individual and paired letters remind us of a leaf falling, connecting that image to the feeling of loneliness.

Dickinson and Cummings' unique use of language makes them memorable. Their work shows how inventive you can be as you develop your own style.

Understanding STYLE

❶ DESCRIBE   Describe the **atmosphere,** or the overall feeling, of the poem "986."

_____

_____

_____

❷ ANALYZE   Why do you think Dickinson used dashes? What effect do they have on the reader, visual or otherwise?

_____

_____

_____

_____

❸ EXPLAIN   Why do you think Dickinson left out a question mark after the phrase, "did you not"?

_____

_____

_____

_____

❹ COMPARE/CONTRAST   Compare Dickinson's style with Cummings' style. How do they differ, and what do they have in common?

_____

_____

_____

_____

_____

5 E.E. Cummings' poem uses letters and words to create a striking visual effect. Dickinson often wrote with dashes and in fragmented phrases. Write a poem about leaves falling, using some of Disckinson's or Cummings' techniques. Write as much or as little as you need to. You do not have to use this entire page, and you can use additional sheets if necessary.

_____

_____

_____

_____

_____

_____

_____

_____

_____

_____

_____

_____

_____

_____

_____

_____

_____

_____

_____

_____

_____

_____

_____

27. SYMBOLISM

The use of images or symbols to represent something more

With symbolism, there is more than meets the eye. A black cat is hardly ever just a black cat, and a rose is hardly ever a rose. These things have ceased to be just *things;* they stand for different ideas and emotions.

Mark Twain creates an unlikely symbol—the food on his characters' plates—in *The Adventures of Huckleberry Finn.* At the beginning of the novel, Huck Finn has been adopted by a well-meaning widow, and he tries to adjust to polite society. When the widow says Grace at mealtimes, Huck thinks to himself:

> *"When you got to the table you couldn't go right to eating, but you had to wait for the widow to tuck down her head and grumble a little over the victuals, though there warn't really anything the matter with them. That is, nothing only everything was cooked by itself. In a barrel of odds and ends it is different; things get mixed up, and the juice kind of swaps around, and the things go better."*

Many readers see "the barrel of odds and ends" as a symbol for Huck's attitude on life. As Huck travels down the Mississippi River, he meets all kinds of people and goes through many different kinds of adventures. Huck is open to everything that comes along. He doesn't separate the various compartments of his life; instead, he lets them blend together. In the end, they "go better" together.

Symbols are often noticeable because of the emphasis the writer will place on them. Even objects that are thought of as mundane are given their moment to shine.

Wallace Stevens' "Thirteen Ways of Looking at a Blackbird" is just that: thirteen short poems about blackbirds. In one of the poems, Stevens writes:

> *"The blackbird whirled in the autumn winds.*
> *It was a small part of the pantomime."*

Because these two lines constitute the whole poem, and because of the title, our attention is drawn to the blackbird. We see a blackbird trying to fly against the wind, and perhaps here it is a symbol for our struggle against the elements of nature. The blackbird is "a small part of the pantomime." "Pantomime" refers to the act of conveying emotions without speaking. Stevens sees the autumn winds and the scenery around which it swirls as a symbol, a pantomime that silently speaks for itself.

Stevens' poem is an example of how a symbol can stand out clearly, yet may be hard to summarize what it represents with just one word. Symbols can stand for many things at one time. In spite of—or because of—the ambiguity that can accompany symbolism, symbols are a powerful literary tool.

Understanding SYMBOLISM

❶ IN YOUR OWN WORDS Refer to the excerpt from *The Adventures of Huckleberry Finn.* Explain how "cooking everything by itself" represents a different worldview than "cooking everything together" does.

_____

_____

_____

_____

_____

❷ ANALYZE What do you think the blackbird stands for in the excerpt from "Thirteen Ways of Looking at a Blackbird"?

_____

_____

_____

_____

_____

_____

❸ APPLY List three symbols that are used in everyday life. Tell what each one symbolizes.

_____

_____

_____

❹ CONSIDER Do you think symbols vary by culture? Or are they universal?

_____

_____

Writing About SYMBOLISM

❺ The Symbolist movement, a movement of late 19th-century poets and writers of fiction, taught that truth can only be expressed in "indirect," non-literal ways, using symbolism and **figurative language.** These indirect methods appeal more to readers' emotions and imaginations than to their rational faculties.

William Butler Yeats was a poet influenced by the Symbolists. In his book *A Vision,* he claims that "poetry moves us because of its symbolism," and he calls for:

> "...a casting out of descriptions of nature for the sake of nature, of the moral law
> for the sake of the moral law....With this change of substance, this return to the
> imagination...we would seek out those wavering, meditative, organic rhythms,
> which are the embodiment of the imagination, that neither desires nor hates, because
> it has done with time, and only wishes to gaze upon some reality, some beauty...."

First, summarize this passage about symbolism and "a return to the imagination" in your own words.

Secondly, do you agree with Yeats that symbolism will better express emotions than will literal, direct language? Why or why not? Write as much or as little as you need to. You do not have to use this entire page, and you can use additional sheets if necessary.

28. THEME

The theme, or topic, is what a poem, story, or novel is about

When someone asks, "Well, what's the book about?" he or she is asking about the theme. A theme gets at the essential meaning of a story, novel, or poem. Each of these can have just one theme, or perhaps a few themes. The poet X.J. Kennedy says that "great short stories, like great symphonies, frequently have more than one theme." This phrase applies to other kinds of writing as well, and just as we often have many important ideas circulating in our minds at once, a poem or a piece of prose can discuss several ideas of equal weight.

One of the themes of John Stenibeck's *The Grapes of Wrath* is that people need to join together in order to change their societies. A character in the novel, Tom Joad, explains this theme to his mother after the death of their friend, Preacher Casy.

> *"I been all day an' all night hidin' alone. Guess who I been thinkin' about? Casy! He talked a lot. Used ta bother me. But now I been thinkin' about what he said, an' I can remember—all of it. Says one time he went out in the wilderness to find his own soul, an' he found he didn' have no soul that was his'n. Says he foun' he jus' got a little piece of a great soul. Says a wilderness ain't no good, 'cause his little piece of a soul wasn't no good 'less it was with the rest, an' was whole. Funny how I remember. Didn' think I was even listenin'. But I know now a fella ain't no good alone."*

The theme of the following text is also one of social commentary.

> *"Before the conquerors came*
> *there was no sin,*
> *no sickness, no aches….*
> *The foreigners stood*
> *the world on its head,*
> *made day become night…."*

> —from "Chilam Balam," a 16th-century Mayan text

The theme of this text is not hard to discover—everything changed for the Mayans after the Spanish came to their land. The world stood "on its head."

Often in literature the theme will not be stated so explicitly as it is in the Mayan text. The reader should not despair, though, because writers leave many clues. Sometimes main characters, or characters who do not even seem that important, will make a statement that goes beyond the confines of the story or poem they are in. Their announcements of the theme often seem prophetic and slightly mysterious.

Writers will also often gear their **figurative language,** their **style,** and the other tools in their writers' tool boxes towards helping the reader uncover the theme of their work. A theme can unite all of the many details in even the longest novel.

Understanding THEME

❶ IN YOUR OWN WORDS Describe the theme of the excerpt from *The Grapes of Wrath.*

_____

_____

❷ ANALYZE Does the language, or **style,** of *The Grapes of Wrath* help to express the theme? If so, how?

_____

_____

_____

_____

❸ YOU DECIDE Do you agree with Steinbeck's message, or theme? Why or why not?

_____

_____

_____

_____

❹ ELEMENTAL CONNECTION Refer to "Chilam Bliam" and the **imagery** in the lines, "The foreigners stood/the world on its head/made day become night...." How do these images help you understand the theme?

_____

_____

_____

_____

5 Think of an idea or a belief that is important to you. Write that idea or belief down. Then write a poem, essay, or short story about that theme. Write as much or as little as you need to. You do not have to use this entire page, and you can use additional sheets if necessary.

_____

_____

_____

_____

_____

_____

_____

_____

_____

_____

_____

_____

_____

_____

_____

_____

_____

_____

_____

_____

_____

_____

29. TONE

How the writer or speaker feels about the subject

When people tell stories, their feelings on the subject usually show through. In writing, that subjectivity isn't always a bad thing; in fact, a writer's attitude, or tone, about the features of a story or poem helps us to understand that writer's purpose and the message he or she wishes to convey.

Joseph Conrad chose his words very carefully in the following passage from *Heart of Darkness*. The main character, Charles Marlow, describes a colonial outpost in the Congo.

> *"I came upon a boiler wallowing in the grass, then found a path leading up the hill. It turned aside for the boulders, and also for an undersized railway-truck lying there on its back with its wheels in the air. One was off. The thing looked as dead as the carcass of some animal. I came upon more pieces of decaying machinery, a stack of rusty rails. To the left a clump of trees made a shady spot, where dark things seemed to stir feebly...."*

"Wallowing," "decaying machinery"—Conrad's feelings about this scene are quite clear. The whole endeavor suffers from idleness and mismanagement. As Conrad continues, his feelings become even clearer.

> *"A heavy and dull detonation shook the ground...and that was all. No change appeared on the face of the rock. They were building a railway. The cliff was not in the way of anything; but this objectless blasting was all the work going on."*

Conrad's tone here offers clues about how he feels about colonialism in general. In the previous passage, we could detect Conrad's feelings about the events of his story, or the **plot.** The tone a writer takes towards his or her characters is very helpful in determining what the author thinks about the **theme,** or main idea, of his or her work.

Stephen Crane's tone towards his characters in the poem "War is Kind" shows how he feels about war.

> *"Do not weep, maiden, for war is kind.*
> *Because your lover threw wild hands toward the sky*
> *And the affrighted steed ran on alone,*
> *Do not weep.*
> *War is kind."*

The title and **imagery** create an ironic tone.

Though writers write from different perspectives, many of which differ dramatically from their own, they still make distinctive marks on their work. By unearthing their feelings, we come to understand their message on a much deeper level.

Understanding TONE

❶ *ANALYZE* In the passage from *Heart of Darkness,* Joseph Conrad says that a railway-truck "looked as dead as the carcass of some animal." Does this **simile** make sense to you? How could a truck be dead like an animal?

_____

_____

_____

_____

❷ *IN YOUR OWN WORDS* Describe Conrad's tone in your own words.

_____

_____

_____

❸ *ELEMENTAL CONNECTION* Think about the **imagery** in the lines from "War is Kind."

> *"Because your lover threw wild hands toward the sky*
> *And the affrighted steed ran on alone…."*

What effect does this image have on readers?

_____

_____

_____

❹ *YOU DECIDE* Verbal **irony** is used when a writer means something other than they say. Is Crane being ironic, or sarcastic, when he says that "War is Kind"? Why or why not?

_____

_____

_____

_____

5 Try rewriting the passage from *Heart of Darkness,* using all of the same details, but with an impartial tone. How does an objective tone have a different effect? Write as much or as little as you need to. You do not have to use this entire page, and you can use additional sheets if necessary.

_____

_____

_____

_____

_____

_____

_____

_____

_____

_____

_____

_____

_____

_____

_____

_____

_____

_____

_____

_____

_____

_____

_____

_____

_____

Made in United States
North Haven, CT
27 September 2024

57999231R00057